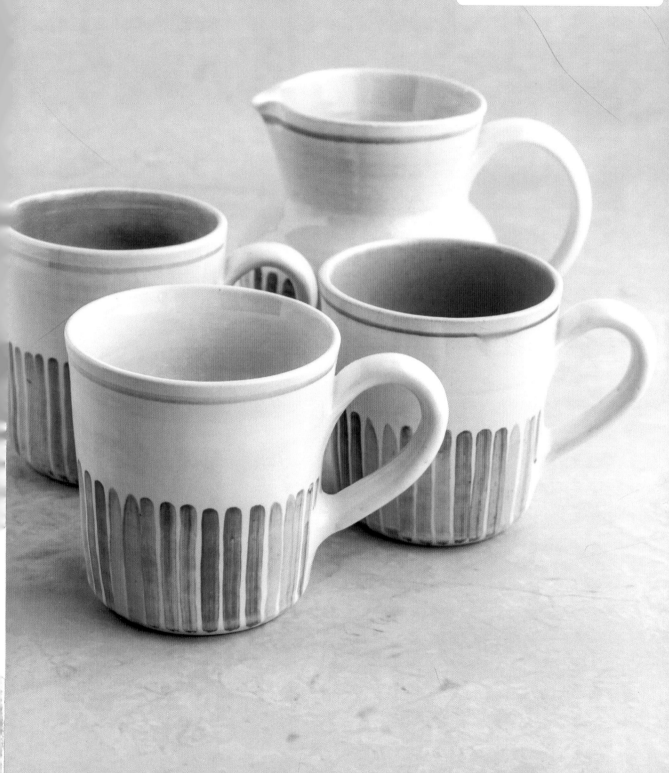

This work is dedicated to the band of
redoubtable women who after the first
great war strove to establish their own
enterprises, and contributed colour
and delight as well as practical wares
to the well-being of our nation.

Forty years
a potter

Dorothy Watson and
The Bridge Pottery, 1921-1961

William Barham.

WILLIAM BARHAM

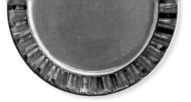

ISBN 978-0-9556290-6-6

Set in Minion 10.5pt

Photographs of Dorothy Watson's pottery © Eula Mickelborg, Purple Plum Photography
All other photographs, family pictures and memorabilia copyrights belong with
the copyright holders, see Picture Credits, p120
Front cover large jug © Eula Mickelborg, Dorothy with pot © unknown; *front cover flap* plates
© Eula Mickelborg; *back cover* lemonade set © Eula Mickelborg, Dorothy packing pottery,
Eb's album © Paul Watson; *back cover flap* author portrait and assorted dishes © Eula Mickelborg

Design © Alison Renno Design. asrenno1@gmail.com
Editors Alan Copps and Anna Foster

Printing Scan-Tech, Hastings

YouByYou Books
Swallow Court
High Halden Road
Biddenden
Kent
TN27 8BD
www.youbyyou.co.uk

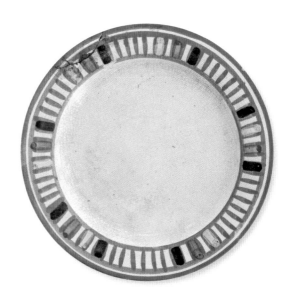

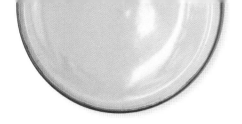

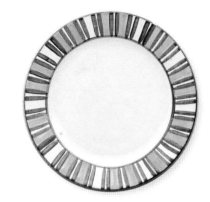

Contents

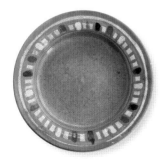

Introduction

I have admired Dorothy Watson's pottery since I first used her lovely large mugs as a child. More recently, I began to gather up pieces from the back of family cupboards and start a small collection. However, my connection with The Bridge Pottery goes deeper than this. For it was my great grandfather, Colonel Arthur Barham of Hole Park in Kent, who befriended Dorothy and helped her set up in nearby Rolvenden in the 1930s. His papers about it are still in the family's possession. My grandparents and parents knew and supported her, and she made for my sister a charming christening mug.

Dorothy Watson started making pots one hundred years ago, joining a small band of studio potters who discarded the Victorian practice of hand painting manufactured items and instead created their own forms and designs. From the start, hers were bold and attractive as well as practical, and she innovated to ensure that they sold. In 1937, *The Times* described her work as "a connecting link between the purely utilitarian and the purely ornamental", a theme represented in her choice of a bridge as her pottery mark. Such was Dorothy's success, that towards the end of her forty years as a potter, she was simply unable to keep up with demand before she retired in 1961.

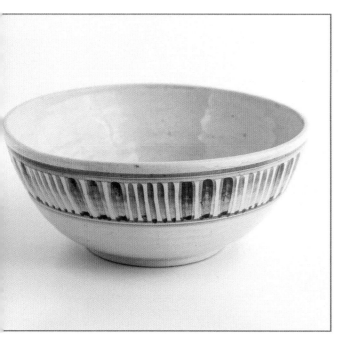 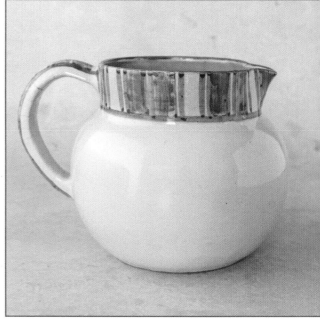

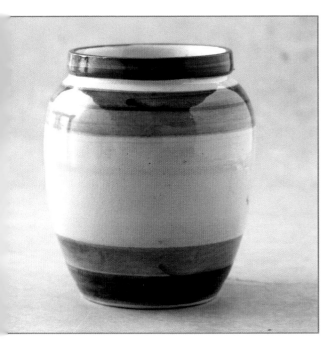
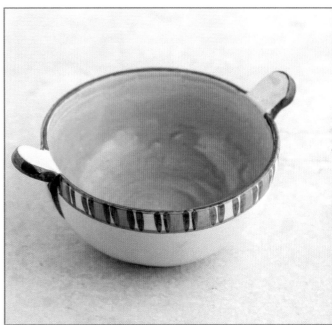

Over time, The Bridge Pottery and Dorothy's achievements have been forgotten and few would now recognise her π pottery mark nor realise the history and struggles of the uncompromising woman who made these fine pieces. *Forty Year a Potter* is an attempt to open a window on Dorothy's life, to appreciate surviving pieces of Bridge pottery and to pay tribute to her most attractive legacy.

When contacting the vendor of a Bridge Pottery saucer for sale a few years ago, I did not realise that it would lead me to her family and to their fascinating collection of photographs, press articles and memorabilia about Dorothy. As luck would have it, her sister Ethel had taken photographs of many family events and left a visual record of the pottery in both Hampshire and Kent in her albums. Dorothy had also left records, describing her childhood and early life in letters to nephews, her wartime years in an unpublished diary, and an account of the Pottery for a sales pamphlet in the 1950s. The more I looked at these, as well as her body of work, the more I realised that her achievements were far greater than just her lovely wares. Dorothy's life had been a struggle to make her mark as a potter and to keep going as a single woman entrepreneur through the difficult decades of the 1920s, '30s, '40s and '50s when many contemporaries fell by the wayside. Dorothy was determined to succeed and did so. Her initiative gained wide attention and her wares, which were as much appreciated for their practicability as their attractiveness, were in constant demand. She adapted through the decades and the story that I have been able to tell is about determination and spirit, despite setbacks and sadness.

William Barham, September 2020

Timeline

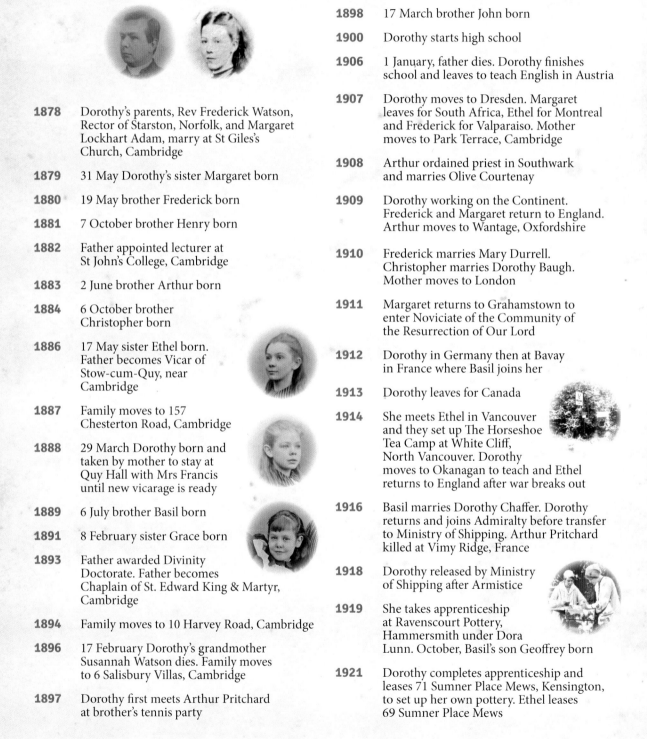

1878   Dorothy's parents, Rev Frederick Watson, Rector of Starston, Norfolk, and Margaret Lockhart Adam, marry at St Giles's Church, Cambridge

1879   31 May Dorothy's sister Margaret born

1880   19 May brother Frederick born

1881   7 October brother Henry born

1882   Father appointed lecturer at St John's College, Cambridge

1883   2 June brother Arthur born

1884   6 October brother Christopher born

1886   17 May sister Ethel born. Father becomes Vicar of Stow-cum-Quy, near Cambridge

1887   Family moves to 157 Chesterton Road, Cambridge

1888   29 March Dorothy born and taken by mother to stay at Quy Hall with Mrs Francis until new vicarage is ready

1889   6 July brother Basil born

1891   8 February sister Grace born

1893   Father awarded Divinity Doctorate. Father becomes Chaplain of St. Edward King & Martyr, Cambridge

1894   Family moves to 10 Harvey Road, Cambridge

1896   17 February Dorothy's grandmother Susannah Watson dies. Family moves to 6 Salisbury Villas, Cambridge

1897   Dorothy first meets Arthur Pritchard at brother's tennis party

1898   17 March brother John born

1900   Dorothy starts high school

1906   1 January, father dies. Dorothy finishes school and leaves to teach English in Austria

1907   Dorothy moves to Dresden. Margaret leaves for South Africa, Ethel for Montreal and Frederick for Valparaiso. Mother moves to Park Terrace, Cambridge

1908   Arthur ordained priest in Southwark and marries Olive Courtenay

1909   Dorothy working on the Continent. Frederick and Margaret return to England. Arthur moves to Wantage, Oxfordshire

1910   Frederick marries Mary Durrell. Christopher marries Dorothy Baugh. Mother moves to London

1911   Margaret returns to Grahamstown to enter Noviciate of the Community of the Resurrection of Our Lord

1912   Dorothy in Germany then at Bavay in France where Basil joins her

1913   Dorothy leaves for Canada

1914   She meets Ethel in Vancouver and they set up The Horseshoe Tea Camp at White Cliff, North Vancouver. Dorothy moves to Okanagan to teach and Ethel returns to England after war breaks out

1916   Basil marries Dorothy Chaffer. Dorothy returns and joins Admiralty before transfer to Ministry of Shipping. Arthur Pritchard killed at Vimy Ridge, France

1918   Dorothy released by Ministry of Shipping after Armistice

1919   She takes apprenticeship at Ravenscourt Pottery, Hammersmith under Dora Lunn. October, Basil's son Geoffrey born

1921   Dorothy completes apprenticeship and leases 71 Sumner Place Mews, Kensington, to set up her own pottery. Ethel leases 69 Sumner Place Mews

1922	Establishes summer stall at Devil's Bridge, near Aberystwyth and adopts 'The Bridge Pottery' title and π pottery mark. Basil's daughter Ursula born. Majel Davidson joins Dorothy as apprentice	**1944**	Nephew Geoffrey Watson marries Kathleen. Christopher appointed Chaplain of Sutton Valence School, near Maidstone
1923	Dorothy begins to supply Heal's in London. Basil dies following surgery	**1945**	After VE Day, Dorothy re-activates pottery
1925	Dorothy purchases 'Wentways' at Beauworth, Hampshire, to re-establish The Bridge Pottery	**1946**	Ethel dies, aged 59. Geoffrey and Kathleen Watson set up Fairwarp Weavers in High Halden
		1947	Frederick dies in Philadelphia, aged 67
1928	Basil's wife Dorothy drowns in accident. Geoffrey and Ursula taken in by Ethel	**1949**	Dorothy renews lease on Lime House and pottery
1929	The Bridge Pottery takes stall at British Industries Fair, Olympia	**1951**	She advertises The Bridge Pottery for sale, but then decides to retain it. Grace comes to live with Dorothy
1933	Dorothy under financial pressure	**1952**	Niece Ursula dies
1934	She closes pottery and moves to Somerset, then goes to live with Ethel in Hampstead	**1954**	Henry dies in Cornwall, aged 73. Grace dies in Hove, aged 72
1935	Wentways sold. Dorothy finds Lime House, Rolvenden and after discussions with Col. Arthur Barham sets up new pottery	**1955**	Dorothy teaches French at Benenden School until 1958
		1957	Maddie Lawrence moves in and helps run pottery
1936	Ethel, Geoffrey and Ursula, with mother, Margaret Lockhart, come to live with Dorothy. Ethel erects weaving shed behind pottery	**1961**	Dorothy hands over pottery to Maddie Lawrence and moves to Oxted, Surrey
1939	September, wartime closure of pottery. Dorothy works at Tenterden Food Control Office and converts pottery into flatlets for refugees	**1962**	She briefly returns to Rolvenden to assist Maddie Lawrence
		1963	Dorothy moves to Lower Froyle, Hampshire, china mending
1940	Arthur dies at Ufford, Northamptonshire, aged 57	**1964**	Margaret dies in Grahamstown, aged 85
1942	Margaret Lockhart dies, aged 86. Ursula joins WRNS and Ethel goes to live with Grace in Chiswick	**1965**	(circa) Dorothy moves to Dashmonden Court, Biddenden
		1968	Dorothy's 80th birthday. Late 1960s, Dorothy moves to Fenton House, Cranbrook. John dies at Kew, aged 70
1943	Christopher ordained priest at St Paul's Cathedral, London	**1970**	Christopher dies, aged 85
		1971	16 April Dorothy dies, aged 83
		1986	Exhibition of The Bridge Pottery for Hampshire Museum Service by nephew Geoffrey Watson in Winchester

Family Tree

Henry Watson (1808-1875)   George Read Adam (1829-1867)
m   *m*
Susannah Clarke (1811-1896)   Margaret Euphemia Lockhart (1820-1876)

Frederick Watson (1844-1906) *m* Margaret Lockhart Adam (1856-1942)

Margaret (1879-1964)
Sister of Mercy

Frederick (1880-1947)
Consul

Henry Adam (1881-1954)
Soldier, Master Mariner

Arthur Lockhart (1883-1940)
Clerk in Holy Orders

Christopher (1884-1970)
Schoolmaster, Clerk in Holy Orders

Ethel Mary (1886-1946)
Schoolmistress, artist

Dorothy (1888-1971)
Studio potter

Basil Lockhart (1889-1923)
Soldier, engineer

Grace Hilda (1891-1954)
Schoolmistress, caterer

John Douglas (1898-1968)
Airman, engineer

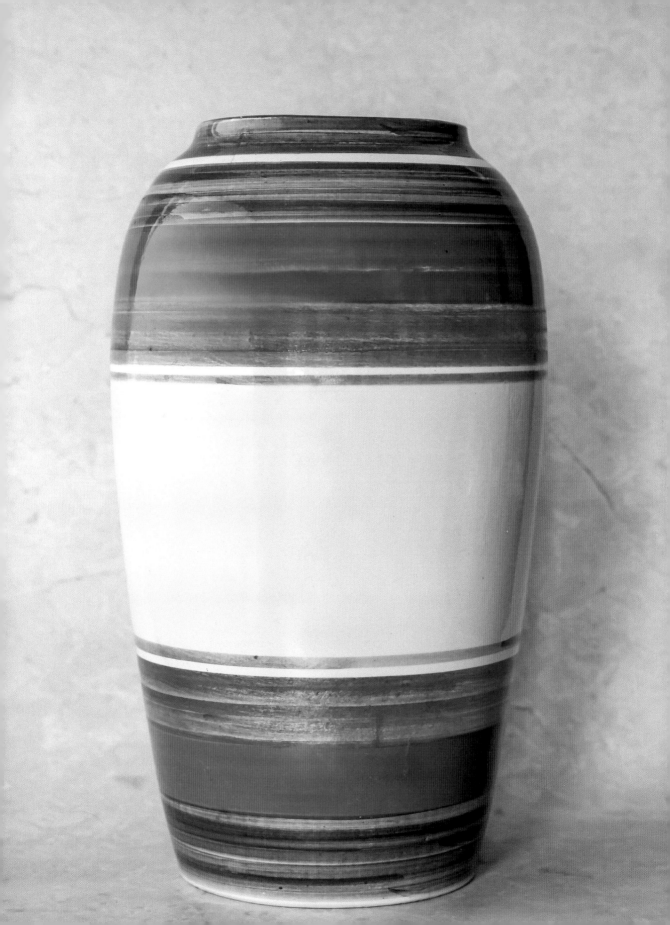

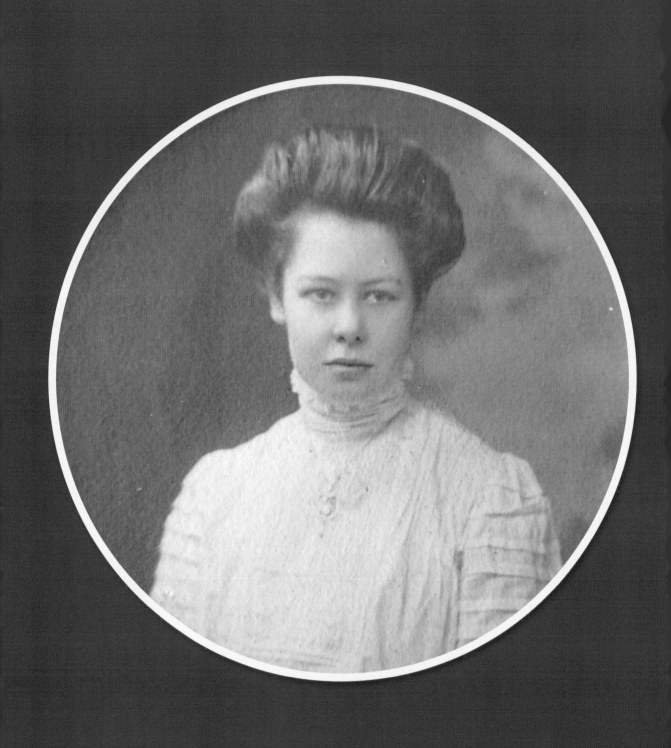

CHAPTER 1

Family and Upbringing

D orothy Watson was born in Cambridge on 29 March 1888. Known affectionately as 'Dod', she was the seventh of ten children and the second youngest of four daughters in her family.

As Dorothy described it, she did not have the most convenient of starts in life. Her parents were moving from Norfolk to the vicarage at Stow-cum-Quy near Cambridge when she was born but had taken temporary lodgings as their new home was not ready. It was bitterly cold, her father was ill and her mother already had her hands full with six children aged from two to nine. However, circumstances soon improved. When Mrs Sarah Francis, the 'Lady of the Manor' at Quy, heard about the addition to her new vicar's family, she took mother and infant into her comfortable home. She was to become a generous Godmother whose legacy many years later helped to determine the course of Dorothy's creative life.

Dorothy was born into a high Anglican family in which her parents' principles of hard work and public service were to determine her own contribution in life. Her father, the Reverend Frederick Watson, had been born in 1844 into a large family in York. He was one of the eight children of Susannah (née Clarke), who came from a farming family in Lincolnshire, and Henry Watson from a prosperous merchant family. Henry had established his own stockbroking business, Henry Watson & Co, and was a director of the York Union Bank.

From St Peter's School in York, Frederick went up to St John's College, Cambridge in 1864 where he gained a first-class award in Mathematics before beginning the traditional study of Hebrew and ancient testaments in preparation for the priesthood. He was awarded several prizes for his scholarship and published his first book on the early Christian debates known as the Ante-Nicene Apologies before 1871 when, aged twenty seven, he was ordained Deacon. His first appointment was Curate to the parish of Stow-cum-Quy where he was to return as Vicar at the time of Dorothy's birth.

◄ **Dorothy in her teenage years**

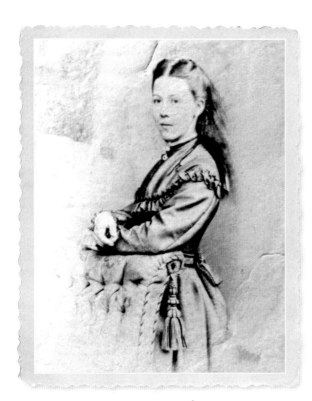

▲ Margaret Lockhart Adam, Dorothy's mother

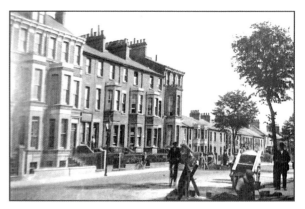

▲ 157 Chesterton Road, Cambridge, Dorothy's birthplace in the central, taller house

In 1878, ten years before Dorothy was born, the Reverend Frederick Watson accepted the living at Starston, near Diss in Norfolk, about sixty miles from Cambridge. Before moving from Cambridge, he met Margaret Lockhart Adam who was twelve years his junior. Her mother, Margaret Euphemia Adam (née Lockhart), was related to an eighteenth-century portrait painter. Her father, the Reverend George Read Adam, was a high church advocate descended from the same stock as the eighteenth-century architects, the Adam brothers. George had devoted his life to building the church of St Mary's, Kilburn in north London, and was incumbent there until his untimely death in 1867 at the age of thirty eight.

Frederick and Margaret were married in Cambridge on 13 August 1878 when Frederick was aged thirty four and Margaret twenty two. Their first child Margaret was born in 1879, followed by Frederick in 1880. Other children followed: Henry in 1881, Arthur in 1883 and Christopher in 1884 before Ethel Mary in 1886 who was known in the family as 'Eb'.

In 1886, Frederick accepted an invitation from the Bishop of Ely to go back to Stow-cum-Quy as Vicar of the Church of St Mary. Dorothy's parents brought fresh life to the village, getting to know and help parishioners and taking an

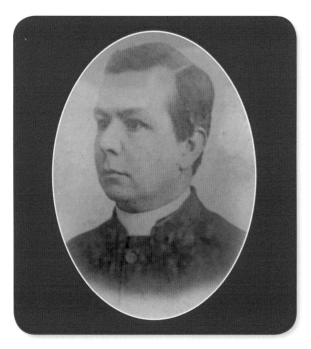

▲ Reverend Canon Frederick Watson, Dorothy's father. This portrait is displayed in the vestry of St. Margaret's Church, Starston

2

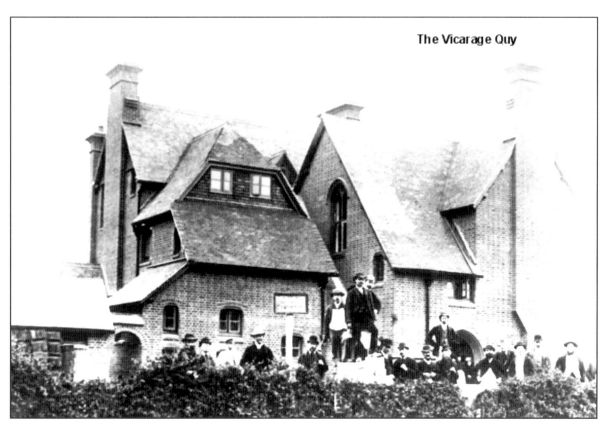

The Vicarage Quy

▲ The Vicarage at Stow-cum-Quy after completion in 1888

interest in its rural activities. They set up a Sunday School, founded a branch of the Mother's Union, introduced Society for the Propagation of the Gospel meetings and arranged an annual party for children starting with a magic lantern show in December 1887. It was at this point, whilst still living in their temporary home at 157 Chesterton Road in Cambridge, that Dorothy was born. She was baptised by her father at St Mary's Church on 10 May and the family moved into their large new Vicarage at 6 Stour Road in Quy when it was completed that summer.

Dorothy wrote that from the start her sister Ethel adored her and they were to be the closest of companions throughout their lives. Two more children arrived whilst the family lived at Quy: Basil Lockhart on 6 July 1889 and Grace Hilda on 8 February 1891. The Census of 1891 listed fifteen

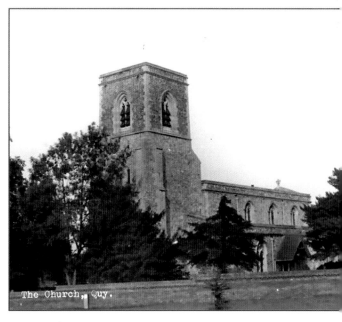

The Church, Quy.

▲ St Mary's Church, Stow-cum-Quy, where Dorothy was baptised

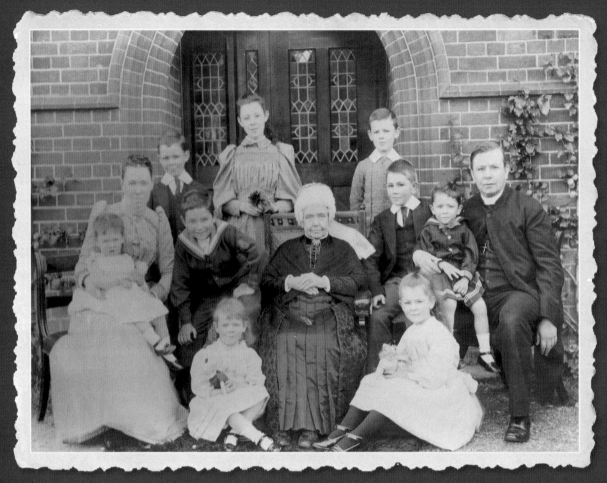

▲ Family group outside the Vicarage at Stow-cum Quy in 1892. Dorothy, aged three years, is sitting on a stool, centre left

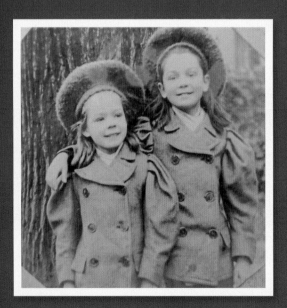

◄ Dorothy (left) and Ethel in 1894, aged six and eight respectively

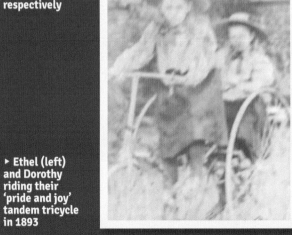

► Ethel (left) and Dorothy riding their 'pride and joy' tandem tricycle in 1893

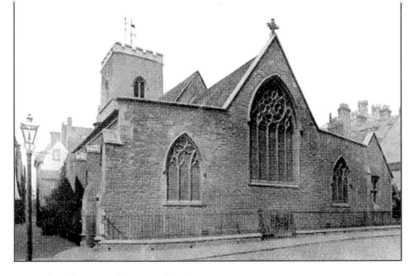

▲ St. Edward King and Martyr Church

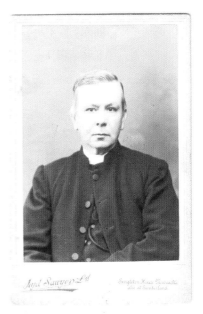

▲ Reverend Canon Frederick Watson, MA DD, circa 1893, when appointed Chaplain of St. Edward King and Martyr Church in Cambridge

people living at the Vicarage: Frederick, Margaret and their nine children whose ages ranged from two months to eleven years, with a cook, nurse and housemaids. Their youngest child John was yet to be born.

From his parish, Dorothy's father took great pleasure in walking five miles through open country to the new Divinity School at St John's, where he was a senior lecturer and held other important posts, in addition to his duties as Vicar. Dorothy's account of her childhood reveals many charming incidents such as the day when her father led her, then aged four, and Ethel by the hand to the village shop where a two-seat tricycle was waiting for them. With great pride they rode home.

In 1893, the Reverend Frederick Watson received his next preferment when he was awarded Doctor of Divinity (DD) by the University and appointed Chaplain to the eleventh-century church of St. Edward King and Martyr in the centre of Cambridge. This brought about another change when Dorothy was aged five, as her father wanted to be near his new parish. They moved to a terraced house at 10 Harvey Road, a broad residential street in the city centre. The house had previously been occupied by Sir Charles Villiers Stanford who was a Professor of Music at the University. Dorothy recalled that many of the nearby houses were lived in by university families and that she knew at least half a dozen children who were later to become famous. These included John Maynard Keynes who was about the same age as her eldest brother Frederick, and who despised her childish activities.

By 1896, when Dorothy was eight, the family had outgrown their house and garden in Harvey Road. They moved to a newly built, detached house at 6 Salisbury Villas on a secluded driveway just off Cambridge's busy Station Road. She wrote that "this time we had a large house and what was more important a really large garden". The property included a covered way running halfway down the

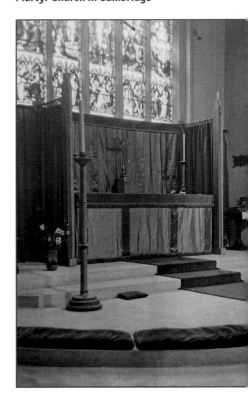

▲ High altar at St. Edward King and Martyr

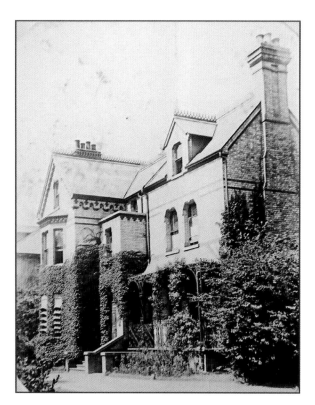

▲ 6 Salisbury Villas, Cambridge, circa 1900

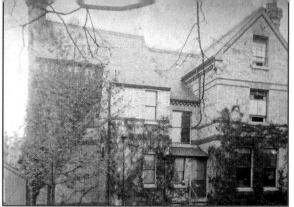

▲ 6 Salisbury Villas from the back garden

nurse and two housemaids.

By now, Dorothy and her sisters were at Cambridge High School and she worked her way up from kindergarten to the top. She wrote:

> At first it was all too easy to be top of my class – I must have had one of the most efficient nursery governesses, but when I got to the middle school, my chief affection was games – hockey, cricket and tennis and my work suffered. One day the Head came in to read our marks to us – I sat smugly thinking I shouldn't come in for much attention, but when she read mine at about 14th in a class of 40, she let me have it strong and hard. I was so surprised that it taught me to take work seriously and how grateful I am that she did. Another factor was a great friendship that I struck up with the daughter of the Master of Caius. She was clever and I was not, but we had a constant fight to beat each other and ended up by being Head-Girl and Second (I was Second). One day we were bicycling down Trumpington St, and I had learnt to ride without my hands. She noticed and said: "If you can do it, so can I" and we both fell off.

garden to a tennis court, a croquet lawn, a large greenhouse, plenty of fruit trees and space for a cow.

As soon as they were old enough, her older brothers were packed off to school. The girls however, aside from Margaret, were kept at home. In the summer holidays when they were all at home, Dorothy's older bothers held large tennis parties and she wrote that on one occasion in 1897, when she was aged nine, one of the players did not turn up. "Ethel and I were up a tree watching. We both played but were too young to join the tournament. However, to fill the gap it was decided one of us should take part and in order not to disappoint either, it was decided we would both partner an agreeable young man – it was then I met the man who was later to become my fiancé."

In 1898 when Dorothy was ten, the family's tenth and final child John Douglas was born. By the next census in 1901 when she was thirteen, her older brothers Henry and Christopher were absent, otherwise the family were together at 6 Salisbury Villas with a cook,

Each summer, the Reverend Watson arranged to take a 'locum' at a suitably large vicarage to give his family a holiday, usually by the sea. Hunstanton on the north Norfolk coast was the scene of many adventures. Dorothy recalled one occasion when their entourage arrived:

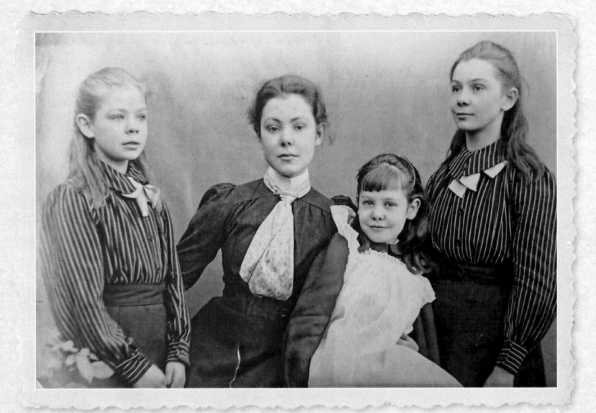

▲ Dorothy (left) and her sisters in 1899

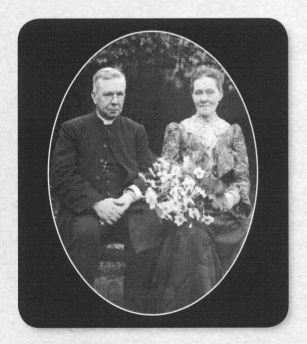

▲ Dorothy's parents celebrated their Silver Wedding in 1903

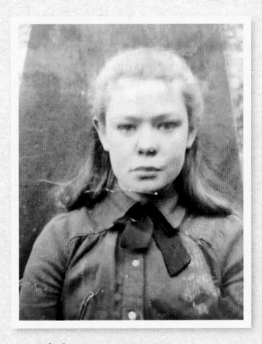

▲ Dorothy in 1903

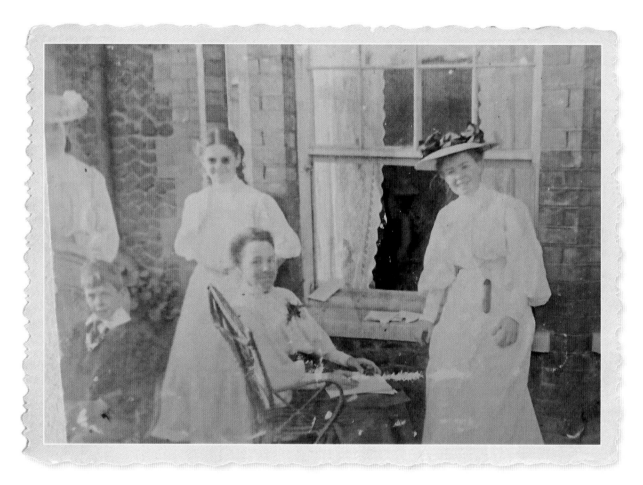

▲ A family holiday
in Hunstanton in 1907

"The railway porter assumed that with so many children we must be a school party and was astonished to learn that we were all one family."

Ethel recorded in her diary that for several months in 1905 their father had been working too hard and was unwell. Over the years he had taken on a great number of responsibilities including a large commitment to the College's missionary parish in Walworth in south-east London. By then he had written and published five theological works, been appointed an Honorary Canon of Ely Cathedral, Examining Chaplain to the Bishop of St Albans and was deeply involved with his parish where on most Sundays three sermons had to be delivered. In latter years he had had to singlehandedly shoulder parish responsibilities without the assistance of a curate. All of this was in addition to his positions at St John's College as Director of Theological Studies, Principal Lecturer in Hebrew and Theology and he also taught Mathematics. He had his large household to oversee as well as taking an interest in each of his ten children.

Towards the end of 1905 Frederick was ordered by his doctor to take a fortnight off over Christmas to recover. With so much resting on Dorothy's father, it was a terrible blow when after breakfast on New Year's Day 1906 he lay down on his study couch and closed his eyes to worldly life. He was sixty six and had been suffering from angina pectoris which Dorothy was later to describe as the 'family disease'. She was then seventeen and still at school.

Just three days later and before the family could have begun to reconcile their loss, Frederick's funeral was held at St Edward's Church and he was buried in a prominent position in the parish plot at Cambridge's Mill Road Cemetery. Unsurprisingly, Dorothy wrote that her father's death came as a great shock; she believed that he had worked himself to death.

Some indication of the standing of the Reverend Canon Frederick Watson DD can be gained from his seven-page obituary in St John's College annual record *The Eagle* of 1906. He was one of Cambridge's most prominent members and his obituary was carried in the national press and provincial newspapers across the land.

Their father's death abruptly ended the charmed and genteel childhood in Cambridge that Dorothy and her siblings had enjoyed. She wrote:

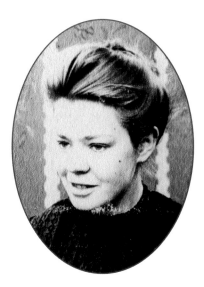

▲ **Dorothy after her father's death in 1906**

'Father's death made a great deal of difference to our family, as it left mother very badly off. However, as he had assisted many parishioners for which he had earned much gratitude, they now took the opportunity to rally round and raise money in his memory so that the boys were able to complete their education.

With fortitude, their mother held the family together, but Frederick's death was a turning point as within six months the children had dispersed. "Mother stayed on at the big house for a bit, and to bring in some pennies she took in a lively and pretty girl as a boarder, who was studying at the Cambridge Art School," wrote Dorothy. This girl was Mary Frances Olive Courtenay, known as Olive, from a family in Aberdeenshire. She had been travelling on the Continent after her own father's death. Although her interests were in needlework and painting, rather than ceramics which Dorothy was later to take up, it is likely that Olive introduced her to some of the creative and entrepreneurial opportunities then emerging for young women. Olive, who arrived in 1907, soon became part of the Watson family when she married Arthur in June 1908.

After finishing school in the summer of 1906, Dorothy left home and set off for the Continent. Probably because it could not be afforded, she had abandoned all ideas of college or university and decided instead to learn languages by working abroad so that she could become a teacher. Firstly, she took a position in Austria to teach English and learn German and by 1907 had moved to live with a Jewish family in Dresden where she helped at a girls' school.

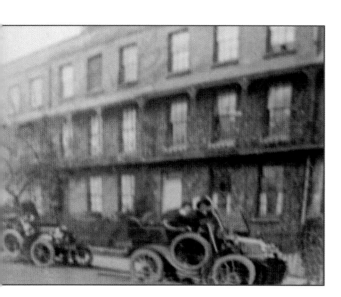

▲ 12 Park Terrace in 1907, Dorothy's final Cambridge family home

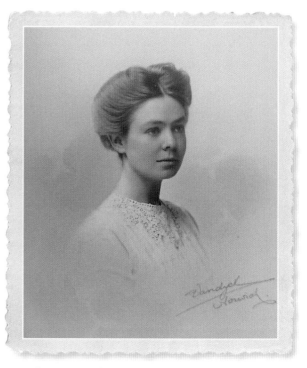

▲ Studio portrait of Dorothy, aged 25, in 1913

From there, she was taken on a climbing holiday in the Saxon mountains and recalled being mistaken for one of the older girls when she chaperoned a party to the opera.

Dorothy returned to Cambridge during the summer of 1907, writing that the house was "full to brimming" with her brothers' friends staying for tennis parties. She had to act as hostess and help keep them all entertained. At some point later in 1907, when her youngest brother John would have been aged ten and away at boarding school, their mother moved to a smaller property at 12 Park Terrace in Cambridge. This was to be the family's final Cambridge home.

At the time of her twenty-first birthday on 29 March 1909, Dorothy came into some money that had been bequeathed by her Godmother from Quy, Mrs Sarah Francis, who had died in 1897. Reflecting on this at the end of her life, Dorothy wrote that by 1909 the £50 she had been left had grown and that she continued to look after the money, only drawing on it later when she had decided on her pottery venture.

Dorothy had become friendly with a family

at Bavay in north-eastern France, close to the Belgian border near Lille. They ran a business manufacturing pulley mechanisms. She looked after their two children and probably returned several times, getting to know them and keeping in touch with succeeding generations throughout her life. In 1912, whilst working for a family at Marburg in Germany, she heard that her French friends sought an Englishman to work in the pulley business after another had walked out. Dorothy quickly wrote to introduce her brother Basil and wrote to him to urge him to accept. Basil was appointed and when she returned to the family in Bavay they were able to go off on excursions together exploring the countryside in Basil's motorbike and sidecar. This was to be of some use to him when he served in that area a few years later as a Signals Officer.

By 1911 the family's dispersal from Cambridge was complete as the census that year reveals that Dorothy's mother, Margaret Lockhart Watson, together with Margaret and Ethel had moved to 31 West Cromwell Road, Kensington in London, where the sisters were listed as students.

Having trained as an artist, Margaret left for Grahamstown in Eastern Cape province in 1911 and entered the Noviciate of The Community of the Resurrection of Our Lord. From then on, Dorothy only saw her when she occasionally returned on leave. By contrast, Ethel and Grace, who Dorothy had been particularly close to during childhood, were to follow similar and overlapping lives: Ethel becoming an artist, teacher and then weaver, working alongside Dorothy in the pottery; Grace becoming a kindergarten teacher before setting up 'Woodland Preserves' to supply fine London stores, then running a guesthouse in Kent before working as a hospital chef. Both sisters were to be among Dorothy's closest companions and lived with her at different times.

As Dorothy had missed going to college after leaving school, at the age of twenty five she considered Girton College in Cambridge, perhaps planning to fund it out of her Godmother's legacy. However, in 1913 she set off in a different direction and joined Ethel who had gone to teach at a girls' school in Montreal, Canada. From there, Dorothy worked her way across Canada taking jobs to pay her way, but never staying put for long. She reached Vancouver in 1914 where she again met up with Ethel who had given up her school job in Montreal.

Together they set up a tea-camp known as 'The Horseshoe Camp' at White Cliff in West Vancouver. This was a success. Although a photograph suggests that the camp was little more than a canvas tent just off the road, their enterprise was close to where the Pacific Great Eastern Railway was constructing a branch line to Horseshoe Bay. The camp attracted a lot of trade from railway workers. The thirsty labourers may have hoped for stronger refreshments than tea, but as family historian Richard Torrance insists: "Dod, although small, was strong willed and that tea would be all the refreshment available!"

▸ Entrance to 'The Horseshoe Camp', White Cliff, British Columbia, with Spruce. A note about their dog on the reverse of the photo says, 'moved – eyes not bandaged'

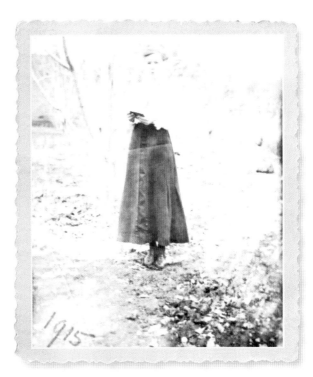

▴ Dorothy in Canada in 1915. This is the photo found in Arthur Prichard's wallet, after he had been killed at Vimy Ridge in 1916

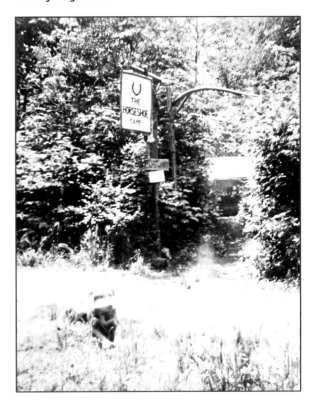

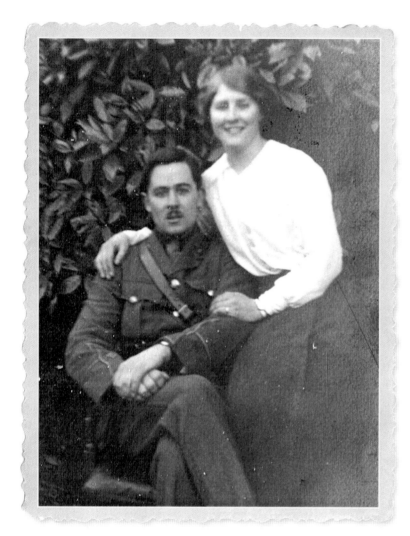

▲ Basil Lockhart Watson and
Dorothy J Chaffer, following
his return from South America
to join the Great War, Christmas
1914 before he left for France

The outbreak of war in July 1914 changed the sisters' lives: Ethel swiftly decided to return to England where it is understood that she volunteered to join the Women's Land Army. Presuming that the conflict would soon be resolved, Dorothy stayed on in British Columbia and went to teach children in Okanagan. However, she wrote that by 1916 the news was so bad that she felt she must go home and do something for her country. She returned to London early that year and stayed with her mother who had gone to live at Winchmore Hill, Enfield, in north London.

Dorothy quickly found work with The Admiralty in a signals department which helped to organise merchant convoys. She was transferred to the new Ministry of Shipping when it was formed the following year in a temporary office structure on the drained lakebed in St James's Park. It may be presumed that Dorothy was to stay in this role until released in late 1918.

Dorothy had written about how, aged nine, she had climbed a tree to watch Arthur Prichard playing tennis with her brothers at the family home in Cambridge, and that she hoped one day he would become her fiancé. Her family, however, felt that her mother did not approve as, despite having been a classics scholar at Cambridge and holding an important post as Private Secretary to the First Commissioner of Works in H.M. Office of Works, Arthur was not a commissioned officer. Dorothy's mother was most protective of her girls and it is uncertain how officially the couple ever became engaged. Their relationship was cruelly cut short in May 1916 when Dorothy was aged twenty eight.

A photograph of her taken in Canada the year before was returned by the British Army from Flanders. Inscribed on the back were the words 'Found in Arthur Prichard's wallet after he was killed at Vimy Ridge 1916'.

The possibility of marriage may not have presented itself again as Dorothy had little money and is likely to have faced her mother's ongoing disapproval about anyone beneath her standing. Of the four sisters, none were to marry. Dorothy attributed this to finding it difficult to live with other people after her childhood experience of such a large family.

After the Great War, Dorothy's brothers all resumed their professional lives as consul, mariner, priest, schoolmaster and engineers. Christopher, Arthur and John were later to reappear in Dorothy's life. But it was the misfortune of her second youngest brother Basil that was to have the most profound impact. Whilst serving in the Great War he married Dorothy Chaffer in Cambridge in early 1916. They had two children: Geoffrey born in 1919 and Ursula in 1922. After leaving the Army in 1919, Basil and his family moved to Birmingham where he worked for the Gas Company. On 4 August 1923, at the age of thirty three, he died suddenly after routine surgery in Birmingham General Hospital. Five years later in 1928, his widow Dorothy also died in a swimming tragedy off Bedruthan Steps, Cornwall, leaving the children orphaned. They became wards of their Aunt Ethel who often took them with her to stay with Dorothy. Later, they were to live with Dorothy after she had moved to Kent.

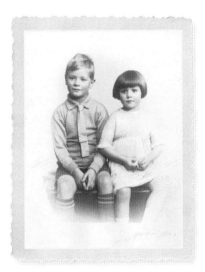

▲ **Geoffrey and Ursula Watson, circa 1925**

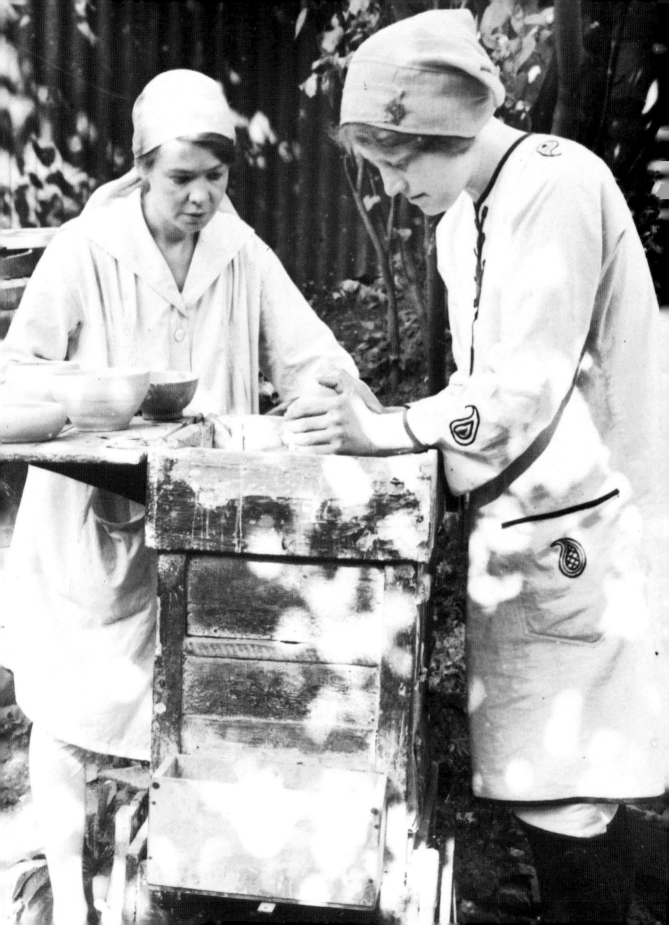

CHAPTER 2

Apprenticeship at Ravenscourt Pottery

When Dorothy was released from her wartime role with the Ministry of Shipping in late 1918, her thoughts were to return to Canada with Ethel. However, she decided that she first needed to acquire a skill. She wrote:

> *By 1919, disillusioned by the futility and destruction of war, I looked around for a career of a creative nature by which I could earn a living. In reply to an advertisement I found myself an apprentice in a small pottery, and during the next two years I learned the rudiments of the craft.*

Having come across the opportunity, Dorothy had the curiosity and drive to grasp it and so she was apprenticed to Dora Lunn, one of a band of independent artist potters who set up small studios in the 1910s to create and sell their own unique forms of hand-thrown and decorated wares. Theirs was to be very different to manufactured goods from the large industrial potteries in Staffordshire, and they hoped to sell to more discerning customers. Seven years older than Dorothy, Dora was the daughter of Richard Lunn who had taught ceramics at the much-respected Camberwell School of Art and the Royal College of Art in London. Along with other innovators including the Martin Brothers at Fulham Pottery in London, and Bernard Leach at St Ives in Cornwall, Dora's father had helped to inspire the 'studio pottery' movement.

◄ **Dora Lunn (right) teaches Dorothy Watson to centre clay on a potter's wheel**

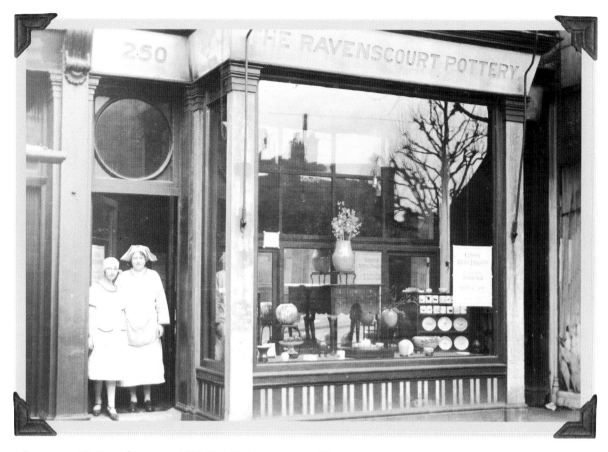

▲ **Ravenscourt Pottery showroom at 250 King Street, Hammersmith, London**

Dora intended to work alongside her father and trained at the Royal College of Art. However, after he unexpectedly died in 1915, she needed to make a new plan and resorted first to teaching at a school. The following year she was able to begin to use her salary to fund her own studio which she set up in a former tailor's workshop off Ravenscourt Avenue. As Dorothy would experience when she similarly set up her own studio pottery on a shoestring a few years later, Dora had to use old packing cases for shelves and second-hand tables as work benches. She had to cast items in moulds because there was no wheel and, without being able to afford any assistants, she had to undertake and master all the stages of pottery making herself.

Dora also made sure that she devoted enough time to develop glazes and decorative styles that would make her wares innovative and distinctive,

as well as commercially successful.

Ravenscourt Pottery became well known but remained small, probably involving no more than seven or eight people at the most, including Dora. Wherever possible she employed girls straight from school and they worked outside in the garden where they could be away from the fumes of the kiln.

Dora's venture attracted considerable attention in the press where it was portrayed as an independent and courageous act on the 'home front' during the First World War. The pottery was a success, but output was hampered by inadequate equipment. In response, Dora also designed her own treadle wheel. She attracted a 'sponsor' who admired her work and provided funds, enabling her to place the business on a sound footing and it was under these circumstances when more help was needed in 1919 that Dorothy Watson was taken on.

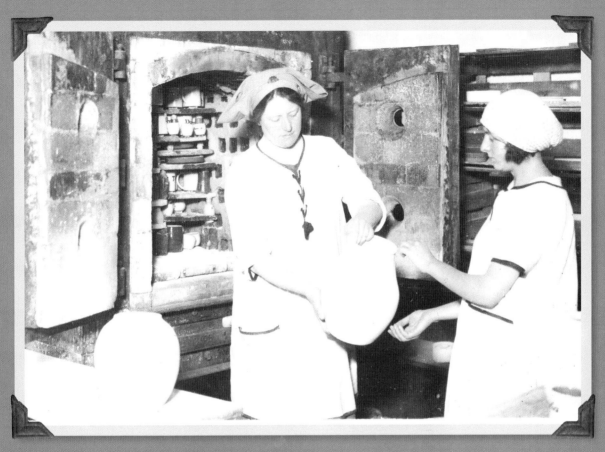

▲ **Careful handling of a larger item at Ravenscourt Pottery**

Photographs illustrate the skills and stages Dorothy worked through under Dora's supervision: First, kneading and wedging the clay before cutting it with a wire into correct usable sizes. Then, shaping the clay into a ball to be thrown with some force onto the disc of a potter's wheel. Next, learning to centre the clay on the spinning disc, using the strength of her forearms and wrists, and lubricating it with 'slip' before applying pressure to raise it into a lighthouse-shaped cone. Then, applying more pressure to lower and raise the cone again to ensure that it was of the right moisture and malleability before inserting fingers into the top to form an initial cylindrical shape. Finally, to form the correct shape, dimensions and consistency for the pots using her fingers.

Much trial and error would have been needed before Dorothy mastered these seemingly easy but, in fact, immensely difficult throwing skills.

The next stage, after the wares had been allowed to dry naturally, was for them to be cut free from boards on which they had been placed using a thin wire. They were then placed on trays in the kiln for their first 'biscuit' firing. This also required placing a tell-tale 'Seger cone' just inside the kiln door within sight of the spy window and keeping an eye on it during firing. These cones collapsed when the correct temperature calculated for each firing was reached.

Having mastered necessary temperature and time parameters for biscuit firing, the potter then needed to let the wares cool over many hours before being unloaded and checked. Rough edges had to be smoothed before pots could be glazed or decorated. Preparing glazes and paints was an area of alchemy that Dorothy needed to master. Paints had to be applied by brush before glazes were poured over the outside or swirled around inside to cover each pot.

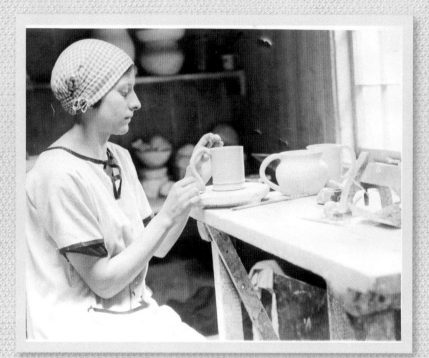

▲ Pottery in
the making
at Ravenscourt
Pottery,
circa 1920

Once decorated, pots were then carefully placed on kiln trays ready for firing again, resting on ceramic stilts to ensure air circulation underneath.

Dorothy would also have worked with the itinerant throwers that Dora engaged to prepare batches of her larger items, understanding their skills and needs. No doubt, she also lent a hand to pack items for shipping, arranged shop displays and discussed sales opportunities, all necessary in preparation for her own pottery venture.

Dora reported that from the outset, Dorothy was interested in producing household wares, which would have been seen as more commercially secure than Dora's artistic commissions. Dora was also innovative in the way she promoted and sold her goods. In 1917, she became the first woman to exhibit at the British Industries Fair, the nation's premier export forum held in London. Her financial backing also allowed her to continue her interest in education. She believed that the way to raise standards of craft in Britain was to improve the quality of teaching. Dora organised courses for pottery teachers and later was to publish her textbook *Pottery in the Making*. With this diversity of skills, not only was Dora able to set up and conduct a flourishing business based on her own innovation, but she was also a talented teacher; a rare combination that was most fortuitous for Dorothy. Dora set out her rationale for pottery design and decoration in *Pottery in the Making* which would seem to encapsulate the values that Dorothy absorbed:

Form and shape are of the first importance …Any decoration, whether in the form of handles, feet or pattern, should add a further dignity and beauty. As a rule, it may be said that simplicity, coupled with fitness of purpose and an understanding of the medium in which one is at work, underlines all good shapes. In fact, the first aim is to make a beautifully shaped pot… before any attempt at decoration.

As Dorothy was aged thirty one when she started at Ravenscourt, and therefore much older and more experienced in life than the school leavers Dora usually took on, a mentoring friendship was forged between them, which was to have a lasting influence. Through the experiences they shared of setting up pottery enterprises on a shoestring and struggling through, despite having very little money at the start, these two women had much in common. Both were determined to prove that they could succeed in the post-war liberated times for women and for a while both did: Dora because pottery was in her blood and she was determined to pursue it as a career in some form or other; Dorothy because she had nothing behind her to fall back on and she was motivated to learn and succeed to provide an income.

When after two years Dorothy left Ravenscourt in 1921 to set up on her own, Dora admiringly recognised her success:

A Miss Dorothy Watson joined us as an apprentice to learn pottery. She did not wish for any but the household section. After leaving she developed her own household pottery which was charming and gay, most suitable for daily needs. The pottery still flourishes and has the name "The Bridge Pottery".

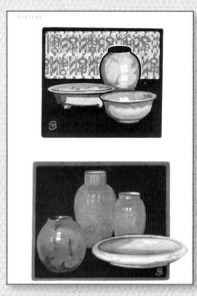

▲ Ravenscourt Pottery artwork by artist Dora Stone from *Studio Magazine*, 1919

Declining interest in Dora's style led to the closure of Ravenscourt Pottery by 1925, about four years after Dorothy had left. However, until then, they were to sell alongside each other at fairs and at Heal's Store in London, and Dorothy later took on the mantle of exhibiting at The British Industries Fair in 1929 after Dora had given up.

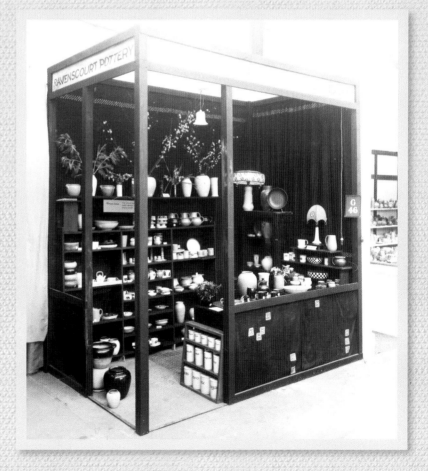

▶ Ravenscourt Pottery stand at a London fair

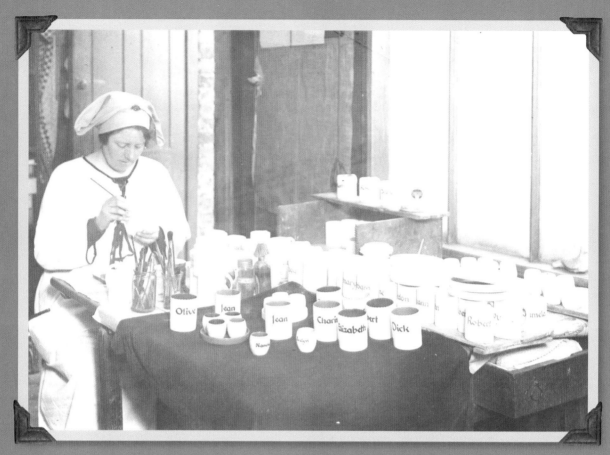

▲ Hand-painting items at Ravenscourt Pottery

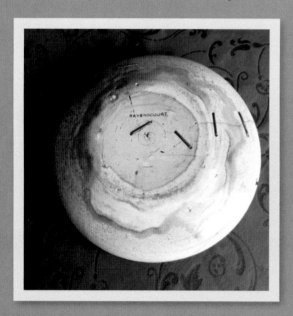

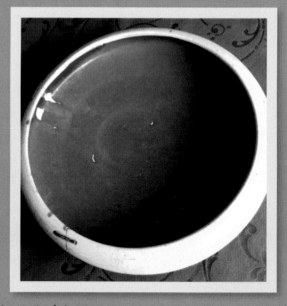

▲ Dorothy's early Ravencourt bowl, handed down through her brother Arthur's family

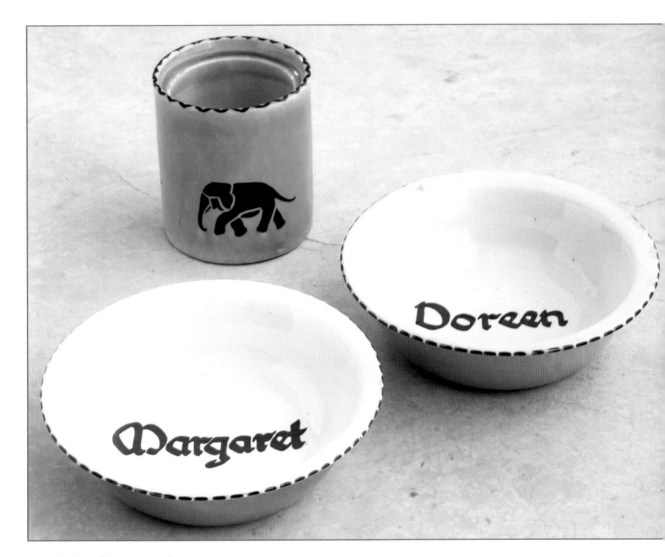

▲ A selection of Ravenscourt Pottery wares

Intriguingly, a large and heavy bowl with a diameter of about 11 inches, glazed in lemon yellow with contrasting cobalt inside, incised 'Ravenscourt' on the base has been passed down through the family of Dorothy's brother Arthur. Given its glazing imperfections and heavy design, there is speculation that this could have been an early trial piece as Dorothy explored household designs at Ravenscourt, using glazes that Dora already had to hand. This could be the earliest known piece of Dorothy's work which she retained.

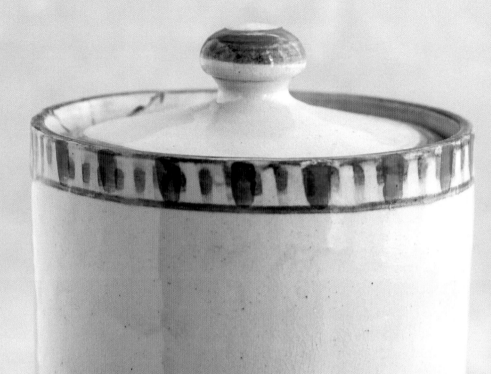
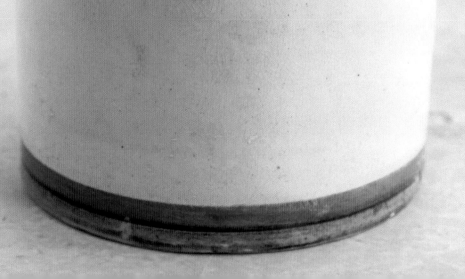

CURRANTS

CHAPTER 3

Sumner Place Mews

After two years apprenticeship under Dora Lunn, Dorothy left Ravenscourt Pottery in 1921. She took a lease on a small cottage and stable at 71 Sumner Place Mews, South Kensington in central London, and set up on her own. Ethel did likewise; installing her weaving loom next door at 69. The sisters lived in improvised flats above, joined by their mother from her Enfield home. John, who had retrained as an engineer after the Armistice, briefly lived with them until he left for Rangoon in March 1922.

From the beginning, Dorothy purchased clay 'ready pugged' from Fulham Pottery and had it delivered to her. Arthur, who had trained as an electrical engineer before entering the priesthood, built her first kiln in the stable and most likely made a treadle wheel for her as well. Dorothy would have used the other, better lit, downstairs rooms for throwing, glazing and painting and her initial task would have been to experiment with it all to get her wares right. They needed to be economical to make, as well as practical and attractive to sell readily. C. H. Brannam and Sons' Barnstaple Pottery was a likely influence for her. Their small, hand-produced ramekins from 1920, with striped exterior decorations and deep inner glazes bear close similarities to some of Dorothy's early work.

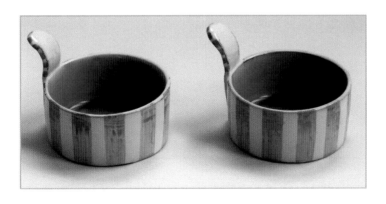

◄ Bridge Pottery currants jar from the early to mid-1920s

► Examples of C. H. Brannam and Sons' Barnstaple Pottery wares from 1920

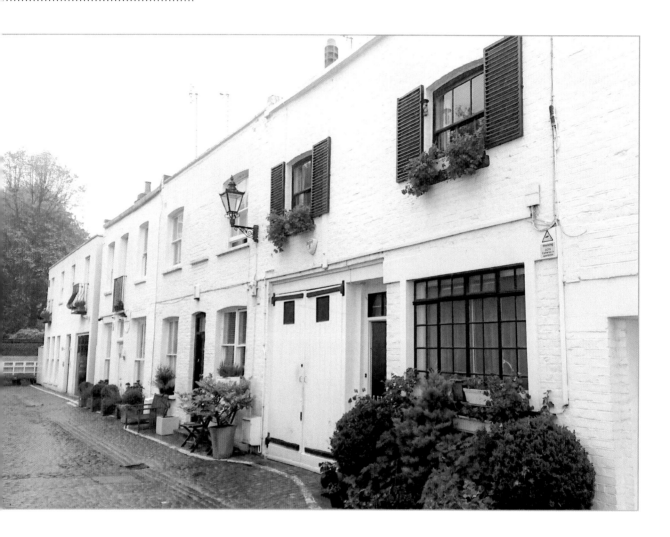

▲ **Sumner Place Mews (with garage doors) with 69 beyond in the cobbled cul-de-sac off Sumner Place, Kensington, in 2017**

She developed and defined her own range in an era when studio potters freely borrowed ideas from each other and adapted and enhanced them in order to make them their own. Her experience at Ravenscourt would have been invaluable.

With supplies to be purchased and all the other set-up costs, Dorothy needed to get her wares to market quickly, but under the terms of her lease, she was not allowed to sell from her mews. Instead, she began by attending local fairs where she would set up her own stall. This was not enough. Dorothy recounted that after several months of strenuous work she came across the idea of selling from a stall at Devil's Bridge near Aberystwyth.

Many famous people such as William Wordsworth had visited and romanticised Devil's Bridge at the top of Rheidol Gorge, about twelve miles into the Cambrian Mountains east of Aberystwyth. The steep gorge, high waterfalls, three stacked bridges and the distinctive Alpine style 'Hafod Hotel' made it a popular attraction. Since 1904 a narrow-gauge railway brought visitors directly up from Aberystwyth which had become a thriving summer resort with smart

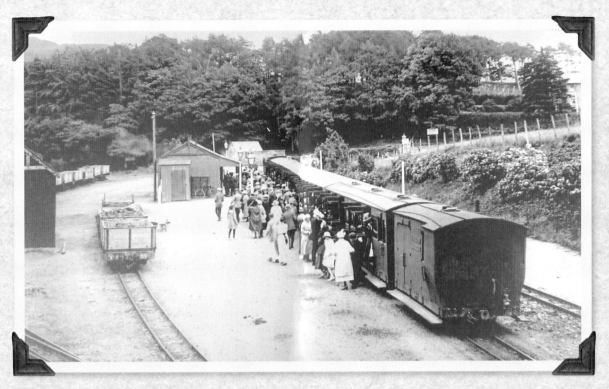

▲ Summer train disgorging tourists at the top station for Devil's Bridge

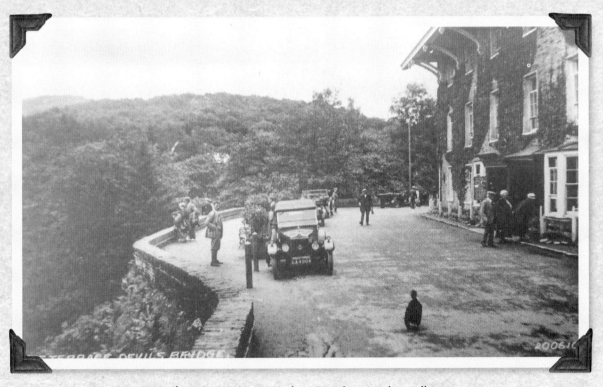

▲ Terrace of the Hafod Hotel, Devil's Bridge, in the 1920s where Dorothy set up her stall

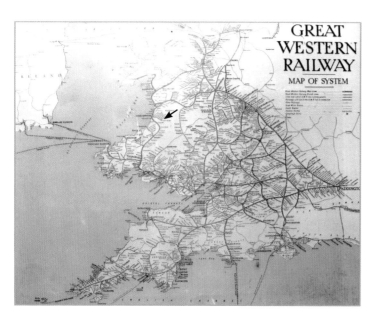

▲ **Great Western Railway map of system, c. 1925, with the narrow-gauge branch line up to Devil's Bridge marked with an arrow**

hotels on the seafront and boarding houses catering for all budgets. Holidaymakers were drawn by the possibility of making mountain excursions as well as visiting beach and coastal attractions. Dorothy had probably been to Aberystwyth and Devil's Bridge earlier and was struck by the opportunity. With throngs of tourists arriving for short visits on the frequent trains, and then being pressed into the compact site with little for them to do other than peer off the bridge and admire the views, selling souvenirs was a sure success.

In 1922, at about the time that Dorothy established her stall there, Great Western Railway took over the narrow-gauge line and began to provide direct services to Aberystwyth from London with the 'Cambrian Coastal Express'.

Thus, although over 260 miles away, Devil's Bridge became readily accessible by train from Paddington Station in London; a journey eased by the assistance of porters and baggage vans to help carry her baskets of wares. Given her travel experience, she would have thought nothing of the distance from London. Dorothy recalled:

> I sent all my wares to Devil's Bridge and set up a roadside stall, attracting the attention of the tourists to this lovely spot by pedalling a home-made potter's wheel. It was a great success and I only wished I had more to sell. They called it "the Pottery by the bridge", hence the name which has often puzzled people.

▲ **Three layers at Devil's Bridge**

Now associated with this landmark, Dorothy adopted a simple representation of the bridge as her pottery mark, which she also described as symbolising a link between utilitarian and ornamental types of pottery. Her pottery mark was either painted or incised on the underside of her wares and was to remain unchanged throughout the existence of The Bridge Pottery. She ensured that the mark, sometimes incorrectly interpreted as a Greek 'pi' sign π, was registered to her and listed in Geoffrey Godden's *Encyclopedia of British Pottery and Porcelain Marks*.

With the Devil's Bridge stall being a summer activity, Dorothy had to find other outlets and she took samples around shops trying to persuade retailers to stock them. Some took them for varying periods, but more importantly, building on links she had made whilst at Ravenscourt, she also began to supply Messrs Heal & Sons Ltd. of Tottenham Court Road, the famous furniture store.

Sir Ambrose Heal, who had taken control of the family firm in 1913, helped to popularise Art Deco in England, having been impressed by Ruskin and Morris and

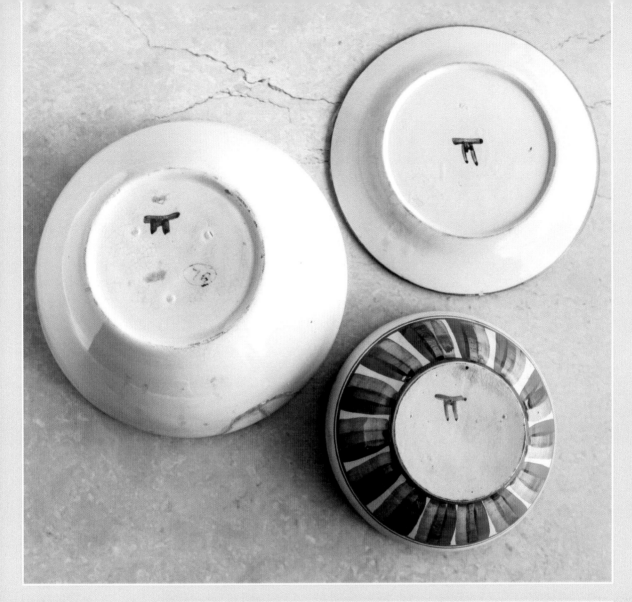

▲ Painted representations of The Bridge Pottery mark

▲ Bridge Pottery mark as entered in *Encyclopaedia of British Pottery and Porcelain Marks*, 1964

Mid-19th century.

Many members of the Briddon family were potting at or near Brampton in the 19th century. A Henry Briddon was still working in the 1880's. The most important Briddon pottery was the Walton Pottery built by the first William Briddon in 1790 and which was continued by two further generations of the same name.

583	S & H BRIDDON	Impressed mark, c. 1848–c. 1860.
BRIDGE		BRIDGE POTTERY (Dorothy Watson), Rolvenden, Kent. Est. 1921 to present day. *Earthenwares*.
584	⊓	Impressed or printed mark, 1921– .
BRIDGE		BRIDGE PRODUCTS CO. (H. C. Swann), Bridge House, Winscombe, Somerset. 1954–63. *Earthenwares*.
585	BP WINSCOMBE SOMERSET	Printed or impressed mark, 1954–63.

BRIDGWOOD

589	BRIDGWOO CLARK
590	B &
590a	B & BURS

BRIDGWOOD

591	BRID
592	S. BI

593

27

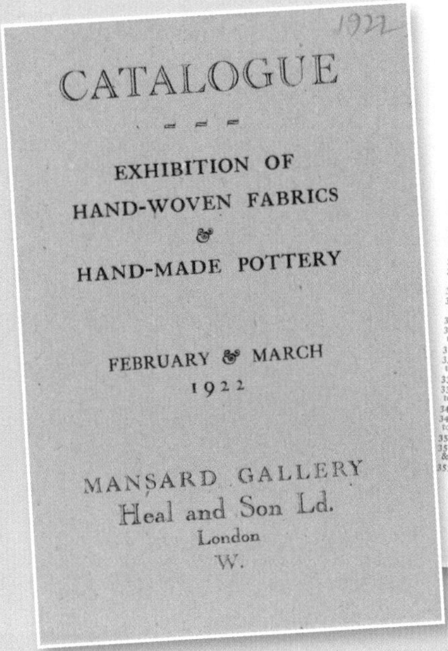

CATALOGUE

- - -

EXHIBITION OF
HAND-WOVEN FABRICS
&
HAND-MADE POTTERY

FEBRUARY & MARCH
1922

MANSARD GALLERY
Heal and Son Ld.
London
W.

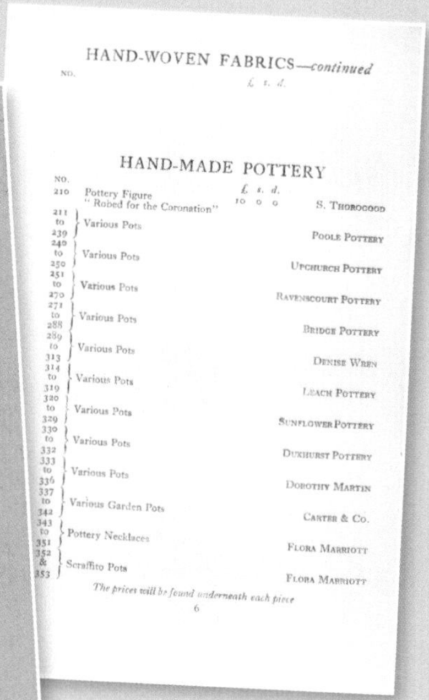

1922

HAND-WOVEN FABRICS—*continued*

NO.   £ s. d.

HAND-MADE POTTERY

NO.		£ s. d.	
210	Pottery Figure "Robed for the Coronation"	10 0 0	S. THOROGOOD
211 to 239	Various Pots		POOLE POTTERY
240 to 250	Various Pots		UPCHURCH POTTERY
251 to 270	Various Pots		RAVENSCOURT POTTERY
271 to 288	Various Pots		BRIDGE POTTERY
289 to 313	Various Pots		DENISE WREN
314 to 319	Various Pots		LEACH POTTERY
320 to 329	Various Pots		SUNFLOWER POTTERY
330 to 332	Various Pots		DIXHURST POTTERY
333 to 336	Various Pots		DOROTHY MARTIN
337 to 342	Various Garden Pots		CANTER & CO.
343 to 351	Pottery Necklaces		FLORA MARRIOTT
352 & 353	Scraffito Pots		FLORA MARRIOTT

The prices will be found underneath each piece

6

was an admirer of the Arts and Crafts Movement. In 1917 the new store designed by Cecil Brewer was opened on Tottenham Court Road. Although it included an attractive spiral staircase to draw people to the upper retail floors, he wanted more reason for customers to go up and had the idea of converting the unused roof space into an exhibition area, the Mansard Gallery. Sir Ambrose was keen to include artist potters in the evolving sequence of Mansard Gallery displays and knew that inviting them in would be an opportunity to create fresh interest in his store through the firm's catalogues and posters. He was also aware of the enormous difficulties for small potters and was concerned that the tradition had nearly been allowed to die out in England.

Dorothy was able to take advantage of the opportunity at Heal's and entered thirty seven items for the Mansard Gallery 'Artist-Potter Exhibition' in early 1922 where they were catalogued alongside Ravenscourt and Poole pottery. This must have brought interest and prestige to the new Bridge Pottery, having its wares displayed at the 'Shop of Adventure', one of London's most important, fashionable and design-conscious stores.

For this initial relationship, which was only to last for six weeks between 15 February and 31 March, her items needed to be brought to the shop by receiving day, about two weeks prior; there being no contract or further commitment on either side. The pottery must have been well received as her relationship with Heal's grew and although her wares were not listed in their main sales catalogues until later, she continued to supply them through an ad-hoc arrangement, week after week. Dorothy wrote:

Messrs Heal and Sons Ltd of Tottenham Court Road were very kind to me. They sent their horse-drawn van to the mews every Friday afternoon and the driver helped me to pack all I had made during the week into it.

Heal & Son's horse-drawn vans, which had been retained during the war from the previous century, soon gave way to larger motorised vehicles converted from wartime ambulances.

Dorothy recalled that this was a time of much hard work, as their arrival every Friday, to be loaded up with the week's output, must have been daunting. In subsequent years the pressure would increase, but for now she cheerfully wrote:

▲ **Heal & Sons Hand-Made Pottery exhibition catalogue, February & March 1922, with Bridge Pottery items listed alongside Ravenscourt Pottery**

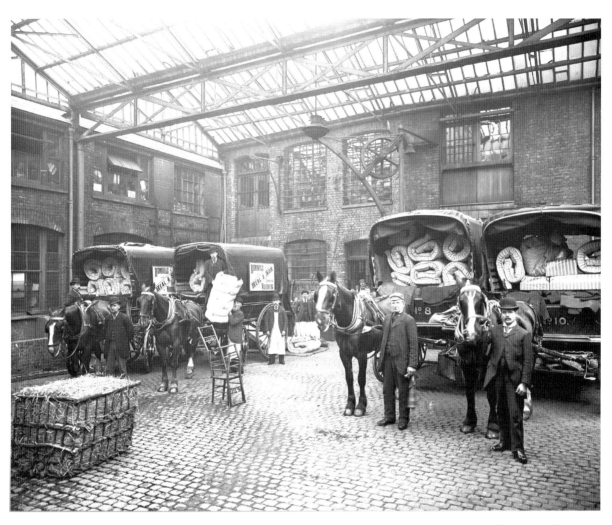

▲ Heal & Son Ltd horse-drawn delivery vans at their depot in Tottenham Court Road, London, 1897, still used to collect Bridge Pottery items from Sumner Place in 1922

The next four years at Sumner Place Mews were busy ones, full of work and pleasure, too. The fare to the West End was 2d. and seats in a Theatre gallery 1/- each!

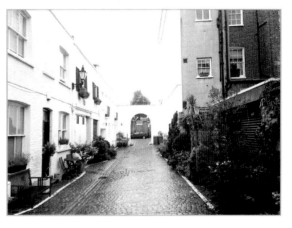

▲ Entrance to Sumner Place Mews, 2017

As well as individual pieces, it is notable that Dorothy sold sets, such as a three-piece cruet set with a pottery tray and four egg cups on their own tray. Later she would produce breakfast sets, with thirteen different items. This may have been her innovation, or again she may have been influenced

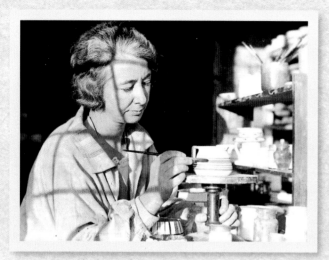

▲ Majel Davidson demonstrates decorating techniques that she shared with Dorothy Watson

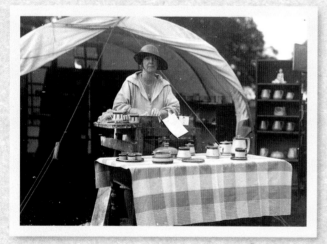

▲ Majel Davidson selling her wares at a roadside or agricultural show, as did Dorothy Watson

by similar sets produced by C. H. Brannam's Barnstaple Pottery at the time. Regardless of how the decision to sell sets came about, they must have greatly helped her takings.

As success grew, Dorothy needed assistance and in the same way that she had worked with and learnt from Dora Lunn at Ravenscourt, it was arranged for Majel Davidson from Aberdeenshire to join her and learn the craft. How the women got in touch is uncertain, but most likely the link was passed on by Dora as her Ravenscourt Pottery was then in decline.

Three years older than Dorothy, Majel was the daughter of an Aberdeen businessman. She had lived in Paris before the war, training in various mediums including art and photography, and achieved high regard as a painter who exhibited at the Salon d'Automne in 1912. With such experience, Majel knew what she wanted from her pottery apprenticeship, especially as she had previously taken pottery classes in Aberdeen as well as at a technical college in Toronto where she went after the Armistice. Something had changed her perspective on the value of fine art to society and she came to London with her rich experiences, having decided that ceramics were now central to her plans.

It is understood that Majel worked with Dorothy between 1922 and 1924 before going home to set up on her own. Majel reflected: "After I returned to this country [from Toronto], I studied with a craft potter in South Kensington and then, having purchased an electric potter's wheel and a gas kiln, came home and set up a one room pottery." However, she found the aspect of her sunless, one-room studio in Aberdeen depressing and with her father's backing, set about designing and building her own ideal pottery. This resulted in the Gushetneuk Pottery being built at Bieldside near Aberdeen, which opened in 1928. Carefully sited near mains water and electricity, Majel triumphantly described her electric kiln and up-to-date equipment as 'non-labour' in contrast to Dorothy's burdensome arrangement. How Dorothy must have wished for the opportunity to design and build her own pottery as well as invest in labour-saving equipment as Majel had been able to. Instead, she made do with her brother's home-made set-up, in a dark, poorly ventilated mews.

Dorothy has been described as Majel's mentor during her pottery period and most likely she visited Dorothy several times in the early 1920s. Not only are there great similarities between the shape, glazes and decorations of Majel's and

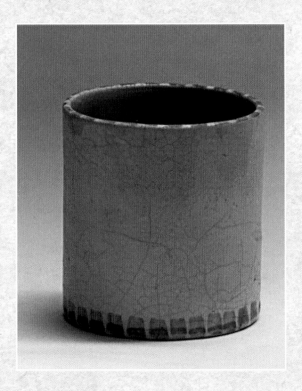

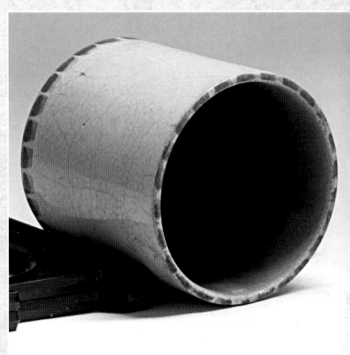

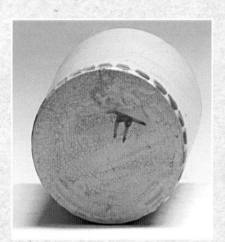

Dorothy's wares, but they used similar topographical images as
their pottery marks: Majel used the Gushetneuk floor plan against
Dorothy's representation of Devil's Bridge.

Majel achieved notable artistic and commercial success before
giving up her pottery about seven years later and turning her
interest to other art forms. Although there were similarities
between Dorothy's and Majel's approach to their craft and they
shared many creative ideas, there was a notable difference between
them, as there had been between Dorothy and Dora Lunn:
Dorothy, with no financial backing to provide a cushion through
lean times had to make her pottery enterprise work, whereas
Majel, with her father's support, was able to develop far broader
and deeper artistic interests. She did not have the same dependency
on sales which allowed her to treat ceramics as one of the varied
art forms that she pursued, and her pottery did not last.

▲ A Bridge
Pottery beaker
from the mid-
1920s, which was
in the possession
of Majel Davidson
in Scotland

Whilst preoccupied with all the demands of her pottery, Dorothy had to cope
with the unexpected tragedy of Basil's death after routine surgery on 4 August 1923.
Perhaps because of this tragedy, as well as a desire to see her family again after illness,
Margaret, who had become Sister Margaret CR following her profession in 1914,
was granted leave to return from the Community of the Resurrection of Our Lord
in Grahamstown. She arrived at Southampton Docks on 3 December 1923 having
given Sumner Place as her address. The sisters and their mother were reunited
in time for Christmas and Margaret did not return for about six months.

In 1924, Dorothy must have pushed her rudimentary mews equipment to

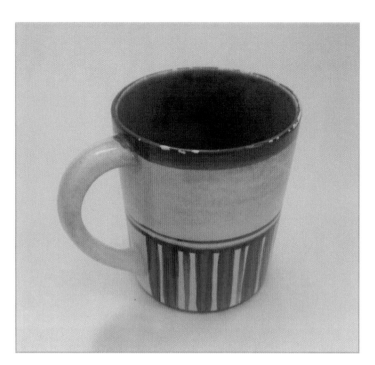

▲ **Bridge Pottery mug from the early 1920s**

the limit to keep up with demand from Heal's and others she needed to supply. She recalled: "The success went to my head, and a fire from an overheated kiln which might have been disastrous, helped to decide me to enlarge my premises." She began to look around and found an affordable property in Hampshire where she invested her capital which by then had grown to £200, to create her own 'pottery ideal' as Majel had been able to.

Thus, after four years in Kensington, in 1925 The Bridge Pottery relocated to Beauworth in Hampshire where she would have the chance of doubling her output, being more efficient and getting her business onto a stable footing.

Before leaving London, Dorothy was asked to contribute to research into pottery practices by the ancient Greeks, to determine if fingerprint patterns left on the base of vases may have been part of a deliberate design or arose from the practice of cutting the pot free from the wheel whilst it was turning. Dorothy was invited by Sir Charles Walston Litt.D. PhD to make various experiments. On 7 February 1925, an article 'Did the precocious Greeks anticipate finger-print identification?' was published with photographs of the vases she had created for the experiment in the prestigious *Illustrated London News*.

In another article, 'Careers for women: Pottery Making', this time for the *Morning Post* which was not published until 13 October 1926, Dorothy was the focus for her contemporary success. The author described the challenges faced in setting up an enterprise from scratch and emphasised the need for artistic and financial discipline in order to survive in her chosen niche between the commercial manufacturers and amateur artistic potters. Dorothy undoubtedly had that discipline as well as strong determination. She was optimistic for her Bridge Pottery. The article must have caused interest as eight days later, on 21 October, it was republished under the banner 'Women as Pottery Manufacturers' in the *Stafford Sentinel* newspaper which conveyed her story to the heart of the British pottery industry.

OCTOBER 13, 1926
CAREERS FOR WOMEN
Pottery Making

Between pottery making as a hobby and pottery making as a business proposition there is a vast amount of hard work. The amateur who has taught herself to produce works admired by her friends, and who suddenly gets bitten with the idea of supporting herself through craft, had better go in for a thorough training as an apprentice as the first step. It takes two years to learn enough about pottery to prevent one losing money heavily the first year one starts on one's own.

As a rule an experienced hand will take a pupil for a small premium: the second year she will probably pay her a weekly wage. Excellent training, too, may be had at night schools, at Camberwell, at the Central School, at Hampstead, and elsewhere.

Capital and Outlay

The single-handed craftswoman should keep things within small dimensions at first, and enlarge the scope of her work as success comes. A kiln that holds, say, fifty small pieces, a kick-wheel can be home made, if there is engineering talent in the family – or an electric wheel, costing about five pounds, and clay that is bought ready "pugged" from a large pottery will set her up. Any shed or outbuilding can be utilised for a pottery, and any available firing may be used for the kiln-wood, coke, coal, gas, oil, or electricity.

Make Necessities!

The beginner must realise that although she might like to emulate Gwen Parnell's little Chelsea figures, or Stella Cruft's models of animals. Or Bernard Leach, or W.S. Murray or Charles Vyse with their beautiful handicraft, she had better stick to everyday cups and plates and salad bowls that are always in demand, if she hopes for financial success. Everyone who can throw clay is not a creative artist. The woman who is making pottery as her career should try for wholesale trade only. Retail sale is scarcely worth-while. She must put her work on an absolute business footing. Shops expect 33½ per cent, and any failure in prompt dispatch of an order may ruin the potter's chance of making good.

The fascination of the art is known to those who practise it. First the clay is thrown and the cup handled; then it is dried, and after its first baking it becomes "biscuit". Now the decoration is put on, and it is glazed by dipping or spraying, fired again, and cooled. It all entails hard work, experience, because playing with a hot kiln is no joke, and the nicest judgement and patience. The conscientious potter may expect to get her expenses the first year, and to see some profit by the end of the second. Amongst the notably successful potters in London is Miss Dorothy Watson, who has lately removed the Bridge Pottery to Hampshire, where she proposes to double her output.

M.G.C.

▲ Careers for Women Pottery Making, *Morning Post*, October 13,1926

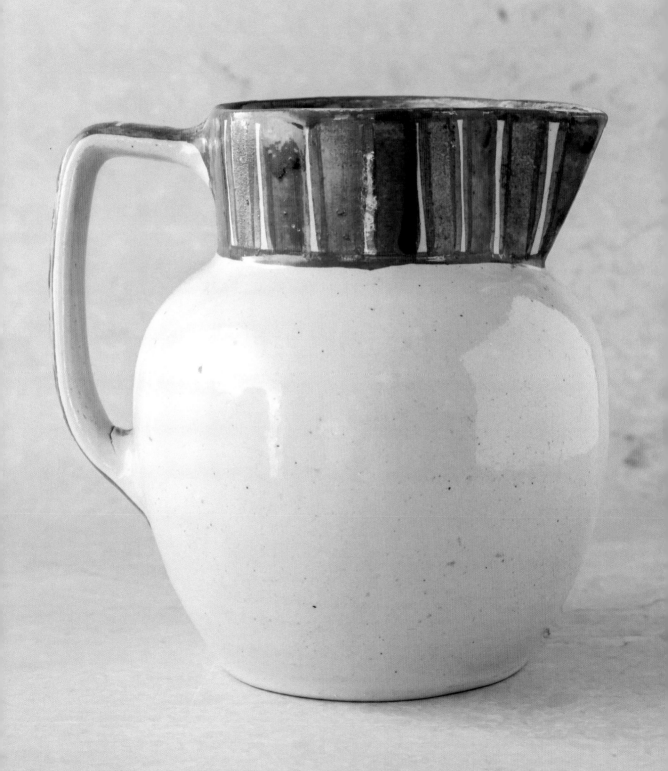

CHAPTER 4

Wentways, Beauworth

Resting amid fields and woods in a shallow valley that rises with the gentle hills, the hamlet of Beauworth is about six miles south-east of Winchester. Dorothy wrote: "I found three delightful thatched-roofed cottages… and bought them for a song, with the help of my friends".

The three 18th-century brick and thatched cottages which together form Wentways had previously been sold at auction in 1904 when they were listed with three bedrooms, a kitchen, washhouse, pantry and store for each. The gardens were enclosed on the roadside by a dwarf brick-and-flint wall. With a total of eighteen rooms, over 260 feet of road frontage and a garden of about half an acre, this was a sizable commitment.

There had previously been a brickmaking pottery in the woods at Shorley just half a mile away and there is some thought that Dorothy chose Beauworth due to its ready availability of clay. However, it is unlikely that the dark brickmaking clay was suitable and so this delightful out-of-the-way location was presumably chosen more for its affordability, than practicality. Nonetheless, it offered fresh air, a charming situation and the opportunity to greatly expand her enterprise after the confines of the Kensington mews. At Wentways, Dorothy had the potential to realise her dream of having a permanent wayside pottery.

◄ Large jug

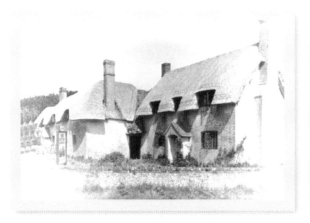

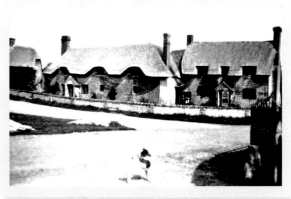

▲ **The pottery at Beauworth in about 1930**

▶ **The three Wentways cottages with tearoom sign in the front doorway to the right**

Dorothy's nephew Geoffrey recalled that the three cottages, two at the front and one behind, were joined at a common 'well room'. Dorothy wrote that one could turn a handle to draw water, but as this was the only water for her pottery and all her living needs, any novelty about this quaint practice is unlikely to have lasted long. The property also lacked mains sewerage and electricity. She described the rudimentary conditions: "Water came from a well – heating and lighting were by oil – transport was there none. The equipment was homemade and often collapsed."

Dorothy kept the larger front cottage as her residence. In the other, front rooms were used for painting and glazing and one became a showroom with cabinet displays. Behind the well room Arthur built three large oil-fired brick kilns. As they needed a great supply of air, he also installed a Petters engine outside to drive a large fan. Well made and well regarded at the time, the Petters petrol/paraffin engine from the Westland works in Yeovil would have run at low revolutions and produced a distinct steam-train-like 'chugging' sound with lots of fumes.

There is no record of the cottages' condition when Dorothy arrived, other than her description that they were 'dilapidated' and she was limited to the amount of repairs that she could immediately do. From early photographs, the lawns and gardens appear to have been in a neglected state, but by the early 1930s the cottages had been rethatched and appeared much tidier.

On many occasions, Dorothy's nephews and nieces came to stay. The family recall the younger ones being put to bed in drawers, and the older siblings being set to work drawing water and putting handles on cups. Geoffrey and Ursula, after they had gone to live with Ethel in 1928, often came during the school holidays. Geoffrey had been sent to St Cuthbert's Preparatory School in Malvern, run by Dorothy's brother, Christopher. Geoffrey slept in a small space above the well room. He wrote:

I went to sleep to the roar of the engine and kilns, which often continued until 2 o'clock in the morning. The firing took around eighteen hours, until a straight cone bent over. Some of the pots were quite large, such as a washbasin and jug and the slop pail. And there were good sized vases. Much of the ware had a pale buff body decorated in bands and lines of blue, turquoise, purple or green. Plates and the interiors of larger pots and vessels were often blue, white or a golden yellow. I made a model of the cottages from clay and glazed it in the usual colours.

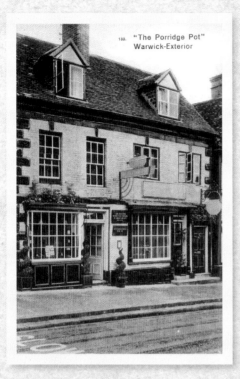

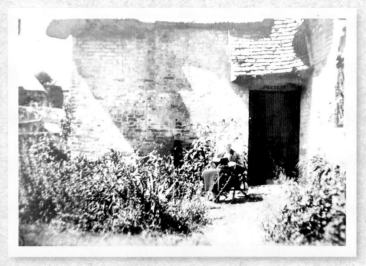

◄ The Porridge Pot in Warwick, to whom Dorothy supplied wares

▲ Margaret Lockhart Watson, Dorothy's mother, outside the pottery entrance

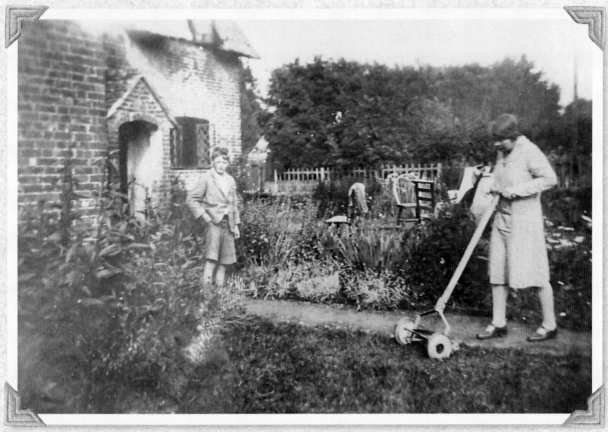

▲ Dorothy cutting the lawn with Geoffrey c. 1932

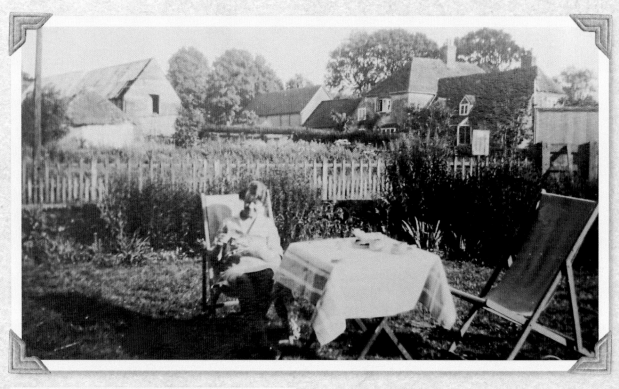

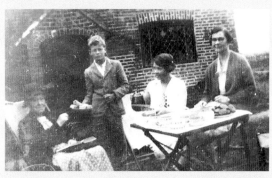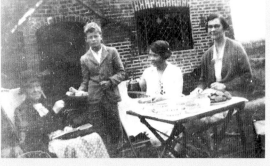

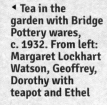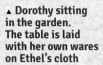

◄ Tea in the garden with Bridge Pottery wares, c. 1932. From left: Margaret Lockhart Watson, Geoffrey, Dorothy with teapot and Ethel

▲ Dorothy sitting in the garden. The table is laid with her own wares on Ethel's cloth

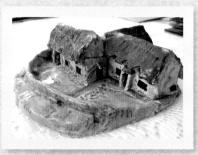

▸ Geoffrey Watson's model of the Wentways cottages

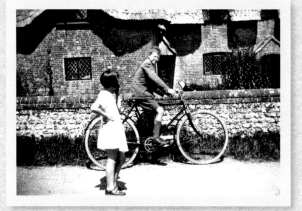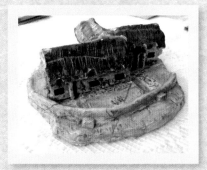

◄ Ursula and Geoffrey Watson outside the pottery, c. 1932

The Beauworth pottery was affectionately known as 'Dot-Wat-Pot' in the village. When in full production, Dorothy threw and turned the smaller wares and took charge of up to five village girls who undertook the painting and glazing. An itinerant thrower, Mr Langley, came in to throw larger items such as washbasins, fruit bowls, jugs and slop buckets. When there was sufficient stock he went on his way, either to be unemployed or to throw flowerpots by hand. There were few comforts for Mr Langley when he stayed. He had to climb a ladder through the trapdoor and sleep in the hot, noisy attic space above the kilns.

Dorothy explained that she overcame the problem of keeping her handmade wares to a uniform shape by employing 'a skilled thrower capable of

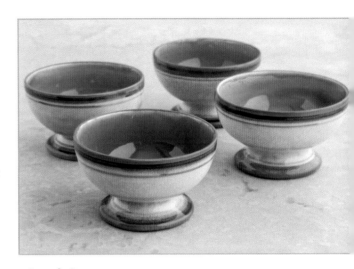

▲ **Grapefruit cups**

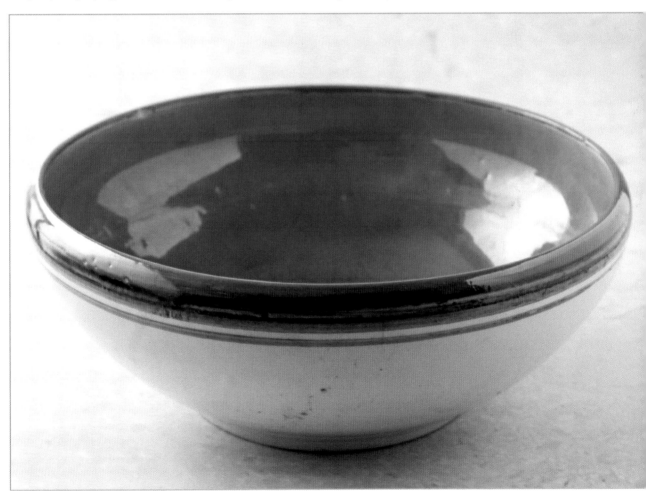

▲ **Fruit bowl**

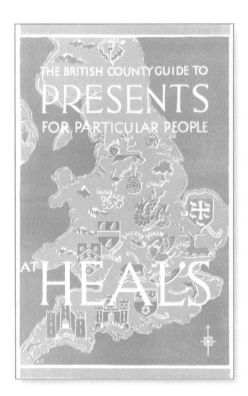

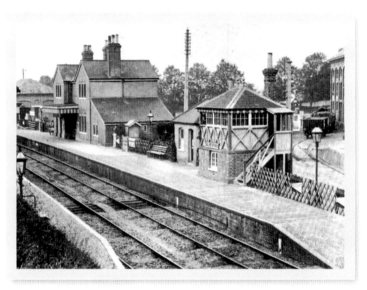

▲ Alresford Railway Station, c. 1930, Dorothy's main line to London

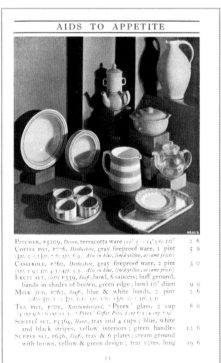

▲ Heal's 'Presents' catalogue, 1931, including Bridge Pottery soufflé set

exact repetition [Mr Langley], and by keeping the works small enough for each piece to come under the direct supervision of the designer [herself].' She established a tearoom in one of the front rooms to entice visitors from the main road, all served on her own wares. Although this added work, it helped to promote the pottery and bring people in, although it is thought that she sold very little pottery to passing trade. It is believed that most of what she produced was to supply London stores. Heal's catalogue for 1931 shows a Bridge Pottery soufflé set along with trays and cups decorated with blue, white and black stripes with yellow interiors and green handles. These were probably just representative of a wider range that she sent up to Tottenham Court Road as more items were displayed in Heal's 'Presents' catalogues in 1931 and 1933.

The tea-room helped to attract interest, and articles about Dorothy and her pottery were published in local and national newspapers including: *The Arts & Crafts Journal, The Hampshire Chronicle, The Hampshire Telegraph and Post, The Daily Mirror* and Portsmouth's *Evening News.*

Her price list for sales at the pottery shows a wide range of items ranging from 1/6 (one shilling and six pence) for an ashtray to £6.10.00 (six pounds and ten shillings) for a 28-piece dinner service for six people. When the pots were ready to be shipped, they were packed in paper, put into wooden boxes and had the lids nailed down. A second-hand car was purchased to take the boxes to Alresford Station about four miles away. Dorothy described it as 'very second-hand'. The railway also provided an important means of receiving heavy bags of ivy-toned clay which she had sent down from Fulham Pottery.

Dorothy continued to take pottery to exhibitions and shows such as the annual one at Hayling Island near Chichester. She was joined by Ethel and Grace with their weaving and preserves, and together they were able to offer afternoon tea sets of tableware, mats and jams.

PRICE LIST

		£ s. d.
Dinner Service (for six people)	28 pieces	6 10 0
Tea Service	18 pieces	3 10 0
Breakfast Service	23 pieces	4 10 0
Breakfast in Bed Set (with handwoven cloth and tray)	17 pieces	2 15 0
Early Morning Tea Set	double	1 1 0
	single	16 6
Fruit Set	13 pieces	2 0 0
Coffee Set (for six people)		1 1 0
Hors d'œuvres Set (5 dishes on ashet)		1 1 0
Soufflé or Custard Set	13 pieces	1 7 6
	7 pieces	17 6
	5 pieces	10 6
Kitchen Set	6 jars	1 15 0
Lemonade Set	7 pieces	1 0 0
	5 pieces	15 6
Casserole or Vegetable Dish		12 6
Flower bowl and stand		12 6
Egg Sets	9/6 —	2 6
Jugs	7/6 —	2 6
Cruet		7 6
Child's Set	5 pieces	10 6

		s. d.
Soup cup and saucer		5 6
Grape fruit cup and saucer		5 0
Toast Rack		5 0
Powder bowls	5/6 —	3 6
Mug (any name)		3 0
Porringer		4 6
Plates	from	2 0
Plate for Soup or Porridge		3 6
Jam Jars	4/6 —	2 6
Vases	12/6 —	2 0
Candlesticks	3/6 and	2 6
Butter Dishes	3/6 and	2 6
Tumbler		2 6
Ash Tray		1 6

Visitors can see over the Pottery on weekdays, 10–5, except Saturdays. The turning to Beauworth is 7 miles from Winchester along the Petersfield Road.

▲ **Bridge Pottery price lists, circa 1933**

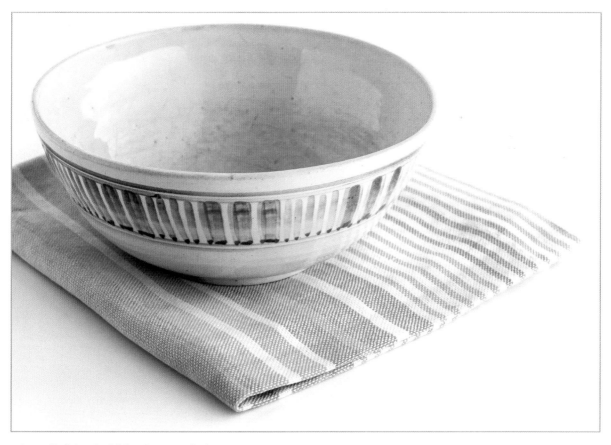

▲ **Large fruit bowl with hand-woven cloth**

The Bridge Pottery, Beauworth, Hants

Dainty Pottery is always a pleasure to see, and the exhibit displayed by the Bridge Pottery, which is in the Handicraft Section, is well worthy of notice, for it includes all kinds of useful and attractive articles.

The ware is all thrown on the wheel, and afterwards painted by hand, thus giving individuality to each piece.

Extreme simplicity of line and shape is aimed at with purity and depth of colour. There may be novelties on show, and one might feel inclined to suggest that those who have to contemplate the giving of wedding presents, might well inspect this ware. There are very few prospective brides who would not welcome a set of this charming pottery for their new home.

(*Hampshire Telegraph and Post*, **Friday, May 29, 1931**)

At the Royal Counties' Show in Berkshire in May 1931, Bridge Pottery wares were on display in the handicraft section.

For the 1932 Sussex County Show in Eastbourne, they distributed cards advertising their presence in the Three Crafts Tent: hand-woven materials, hand-thrown pottery and home-made jam. Of the stores she supplied, The Porridge Pot in Warwick sold her pottery alongside Poole, advertising them as 'very pleasant gifts'. The Old Oak Gallery in Royal Leamington Spa also sold Bridge Pottery wares together with weaving, jewellery and woodcrafts.

▸ **Sussex County Show, Eastbourne, Three Crafts Tent, 1932**

SUSSEX COUNTY SHOW,
EASTBOURNE.

Wed. & Thurs., June 22nd & 23rd. 1932

THREE CRAFTS TENT

STAND No. 72.

| ETHEL WATSON, | DOROTHY WATSON, | GRACE WATSON, |
| Hand-woven Materials. | Hand-thrown Pottery. | Home-made Preserves. |

▾ **Soup or porridge bowl**

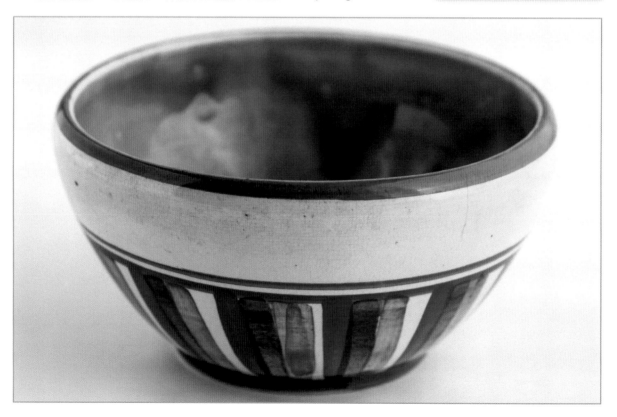

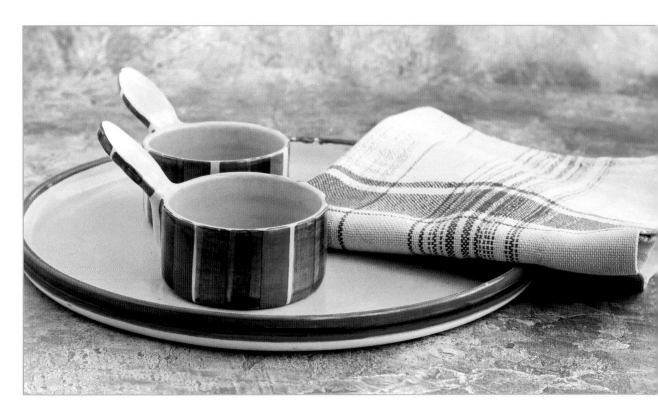

▲ Egg or custard set (part of)

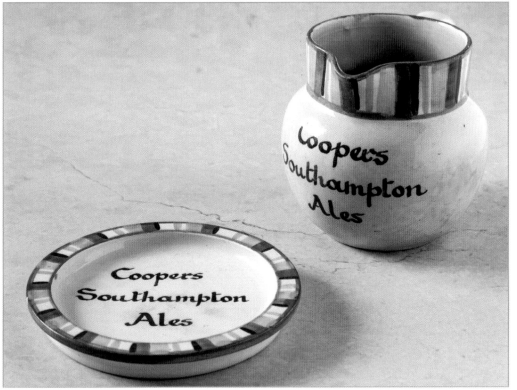

◄ Jug and platter for Coopers Southampton Ales

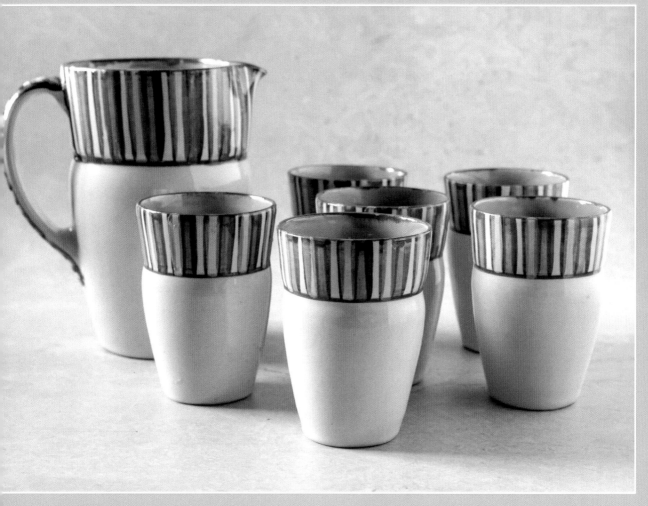

▲ Lemonade set

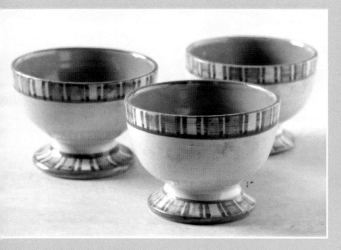

▲ Grapefruit cups

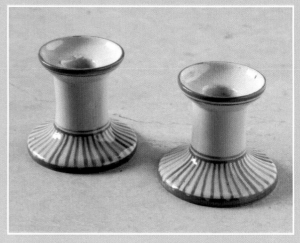

▲ Candlesticks

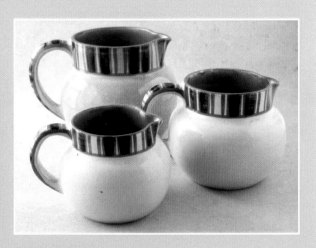

▲ Water jug set

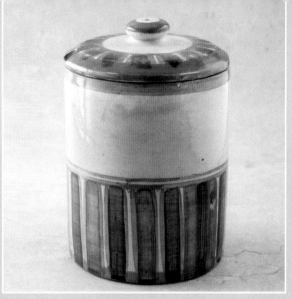

▲ Jam jar

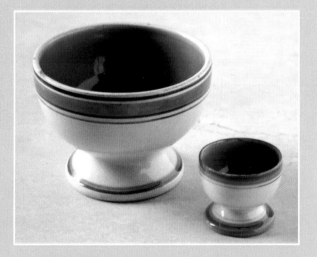

▲ Grapefruit and egg cups

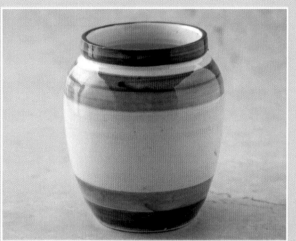

▲ Flower vase

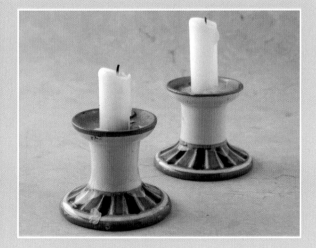

▲ Candlesticks

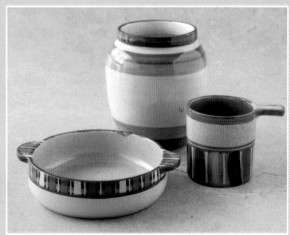

▲ Assorted wares

45

**"HAMPSHIRE CHRONICLE"
8th August,1931.**

AN INTERESTING SPOT NEAR WINCHESTER.

I wonder how many people know of the little pottery which is tucked away in a tiny village called Beauworth, seven miles south-east of Winchester?

Here an interesting work is being carried on, for entirely modern pottery is produced by the primitive methods of this most ancient of crafts.

No attempt is made to copy the work of the ancients, though inspiration is derived from them, but simple modern shapes with a harmonious blending of bright colourings form the basis of the work.

On the day I visited Beauworth, pottery was being made in what seemed ideal conditions. The sun was shining, and the three old cottages which have been made into the pottery formed a charming background. Two girls were sitting in the sun putting on handles and chatting as they worked, whilst indoors a "thrower" was fashioning pots on the wheel as if by magic, and other girls were engaged in painting, glazing, and kiln filling.

The processes were shown to me and explained with the utmost candour, each worker showing real personal interest, and then I was taken to a low oak beamed room where a display of pots was to be found, and which could be purchased if desired.

An added attraction to my mind was the hand-woven curtains, table cloths. &c., which made such a perfect setting for the pottery.

The buildings alone are well worth a visit, and the pottery is fascinating. You will be welcomed and shown round on any week-day between 10 and 5, except Saturday afternoon. which is given over to cleaning, I am told.

Take the Winchester-Petersfield road and turn off about seven miles from Winchester to reach Be-a-worth, as the old spelling rightly has it—" the village of the bees."

T. P.

Hampshire Chronicle Review, 8 August 1931

Always enterprising, Dorothy took on commissions for individual pieces and commemorative items and, as an example, there is a report in *The Hampshire Telegraph and Post* of an inscribed bowl being presented to 'Mr and Miss Elliott, in grateful appreciation, from the Liphook Folk Dancers'.

Mr John Corbett, proprietor of the long-established Southampton brewers William Cooper & Co, lived in Beauworth and was keen to support her. He commissioned Dorothy to make sets of jugs and serving dishes for use in their public houses around Hampshire which totalled about seventy at the time.

During the Beauworth period, Dorothy's wares were characterised by her uniformly produced practical shapes, strong decorations and bold interior glazes. Her work was often decorated with circular bands of colours around the rim and base, or more time-consuming stripes or panels. Some of the bowls were substantially sized at over 12½" wide and 5½" tall for a wash bowl, and 8" tall and 8" wide for a slop bucket which came with a wicker handle and lid.

The attractiveness of her set-up at Beauworth, as well as Dorothy's skill at gaining complimentary press coverage belie the difficulties she faced. She knew that with her combination of poor equipment, dilapidated premises and difficult conditions, she was in trouble from the day she moved: 'The equipment was home-made and often collapsed … and although I had a staff of five and a traveller on the road, the profits were negligible'. Despite a great deal of success in terms of the attractiveness and demand for what she made, her enterprise was struggling to be viable in the difficult years of the late 1920s and early 1930s. An indication of the sort of uncertainties she had to cope with, that were well beyond her control, came from Heal's sudden announcement in September 1926 of a 10% price rise for the handmade pottery, due to rises in the price of fuel.

Perhaps because of the need to try to break out from her financial difficulties by raising her profile within the trade, Dorothy took a stall at the Board of Trade's British Industries Fair

THE ARTS & CRAFTS JOURNAL
We visit the Bridge Pottery

The ancient craft of hand-made pottery has found unique expression in modern day life in the tiny village of Beauworth, hidden away in the fold of the Hampshire downs. There, Miss Dorothy Watson has established a small, but eminently practical, plant for the production of wares both beautiful and useful.

Three old-world cottages, opening in and out of one-another, with thatched roofs and quaintly crooked oak beams, form a sympathetic setting for her picturesque work. The country quiet is scarcely disturbed by the turn of the potter's wheel, the coming and going of the village girls to their tasks of painting and glazing, and the throb of the little engine valiantly discharging its task of governing the oil burners used for firing the kilns.

Miss Watson faced the difficulties of a pioneer in her particular line, but has succeeded in developing a sound and steadily growing business. From the first her pottery was received with enthusiasm and interest due to its simplicity of design and brilliant colouring. The chief problem lay in finding a mean between the artist's work and a factory-made product. This was solved by employing a skilled thrower capable of exact repetition, and by keeping the works small enough for each piece to come under the direct supervision of the designer. Every item produced in this small factory has definite use and, as far as possible, is the best shape for its specific purpose. The finished products include single and double tea sets, after dinner coffees, soufflé, soup-tubs and egg sets, all on matching trays; also a wide range of vases, flower bowls, the very popular jug in all sizes, and numerous other attractive pieces of table-ware.

Beauworth is reached from Winchester by taking the Petersfield road for about seven miles and turning to the right at the cross-road sign. Miss Watson has always made a welcome for visitors who are interested to see the work in progress. Craft shops needing something novel in design and of universal appeal might well write for a price list, or, better still, combine business with pleasure by paying a visit to the Bridge Pottery.

at Shepherd's Bush in London in 1929. This had become an annual display by British and Commonwealth manufacturers to promote home and export sales and she had gained experience there before with Dora Lunn. Among 1,456 exhibitors from a wide range of industries, the Pottery & Glass Section was larger than ever. Dorothy's stand at E 8 in a linking section between main halls was conveniently placed just by the main restaurant and listed as 'Bridge Pottery of Beauworth, Alresford, Hampshire, Manufacturers of Pottery, useful and ornamental ware in simple designs and clear coloring'.

As the proprietor of a small studio pottery it was brave of her to attend alongside the established industrial potteries because, as she was to find out, the fair had become more of an opportunity for commercial manufacturers to negotiate with wholesale buyers than a showcase for artists to exhibit their wares. Of the seventy-five pottery exhibitors, most were manufacturing companies and very few were studio potteries. Of those that were, such as C. H. Brannam's Barnstaple Pottery, they had almost all become limited companies by 1929. The commercial world had moved on from her experience seven or eight years

▲ 'We visit The Bridge Pottery', *The Arts & Crafts Journal*

47

previously when she had attended on behalf of Ravenscourt Pottery. An industry review commented on the contrast between trade buyers who had the fair to themselves for most of the day, and the general public, who Dorothy was best placed to sell to, who were only allowed entry at 4.30pm. Many a problem arose from the public expecting to

▶ 'A Hampshire Pottery in Historic Surroundings', *The Evening News and Southern Daily Mail*

▼ Breakfast set

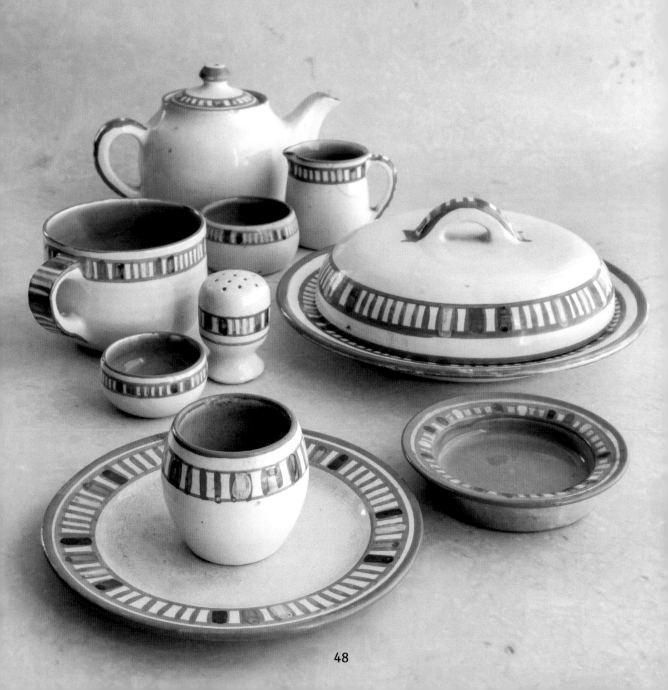

A HAMPSHIRE POTTERY IN HISTORIC SURROUNDINGS
Factory in Seventeenth Century Cottages

One of the features of Beauworth, the pretty Hampshire village which lies a few-miles south-east of Winchester, is the pottery which is owned and worked by Miss Dorothy Watson.

Miss Watson began pottery work just after the War from a desire to create where there had been so much demolition.

She began in London in an old mews, having first learned the whole of the phases of the industry in small pottery. It was her endeavour to make something attractive and at the same time useful, and this has always been her aim. How well she has succeeded can be realised by a tour of her workshops, which are open to the public at specified hours.

It was when the venture had proved too progressive for the limited accommodation in London that Miss Watson came to Beauworth. That was six years ego. The work is now carried on in three picturesque Seventeenth-Century cottages, one of which serves as Miss Watson's house, while the other two arc used as workshops.

The pottery gives work to a staff of five or six persons, but the nature of the work is so individual that it is unlikely that further enlargement will take place.

"I should not like it to become over commercialised," Miss Watson explained, "although, of course, we come under the Factory Act.

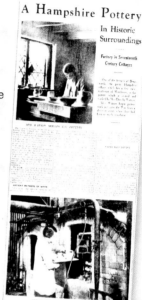

Ancient methods of work

"We follow the ancient methods of pottery making and 'throw' our pieces, as opposed to moulding them. Painting is done by hand, and designs are very simple. We don't copy from the ancients. I am interested in having something quaint and nice. Any copy is rather poor."

The chief products are domestic ware, and while the designs of all the Beauworth pottery are extremely attractive, usefulness has been co-factor in their manufacture. Early morning tea-sets, coffee-sets, souffle sets, jelly sets, broth sets and hors d'oeuvre sets. The produce is sent to London shops.

Miss Watson explained that she followed the system of leadless glazes, so that there was no fear of the staff contracting tuberculosis from lead-poisoning, which was said to happen in some potteries.

A jug was quickly fashioned by Miss Watson on the throwing machine, and she explained that when the clay was half dry the handle would be affixed. Later, when it was quite dry the bisque would be ready for the kilns, where it would be fired twice for 11 hours, with cooling intervals of 48 hours.

Miss Watson is an expert at all phases of pottery work. She employs a professional "thrower" and has trained her staff of local girls in the various departments of the pottery.

Three busy sisters

For some years the Beauworth ware has attracted a good deal of attention at the British Industries Exhibition Olympia, and Miss Watson's pottery must lie amongst the most picturesque in the country. The position of the place of manufacture is artistic, and the outcome is produced by an intelligent blend of the ancient and the modern.

The "thrower," for instance, is worked by pedal, as the ancient potters worked, but the three kilns are heated by the latest oil-fuel machines.

Miss Watson has two sisters whose wares are also to be seen in the showroom. Miss Ethel Watson, whose workshop is at Hampstead, is the creator of dainty handwoven materials, such as tea cloths, etc., and Miss Grace Watson makes jams near Uckfield, Sussex – **E.T.S.**

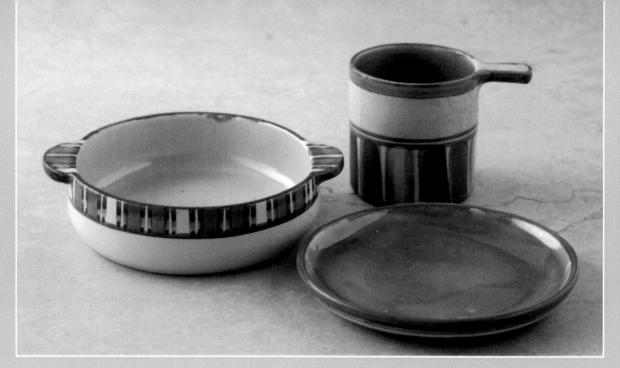

▲ Dorothy's strong and attractive designs from the 1930s

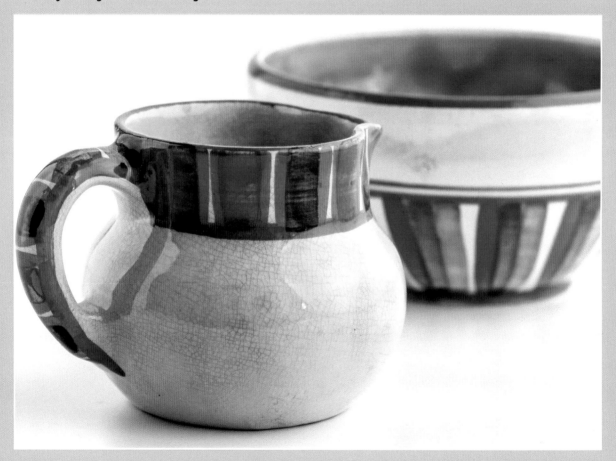

▲ Jug and bowl

purchase at the trade prices displayed when they thronged the Pottery section. It is not known how, with her limited capacity, Dorothy fared but there is no evidence that she attracted significant sales.

Her attendance at the fair which lasted from 18 February to 1 March was a large commitment, but perhaps she hoped that by being alongside prominent manufacturers, she might secure the interest or financial backing to enable her to invest as Dora and Majel had had the good fortune to do. No such opening occurred and instead she was damned by faint praise in the trade mouthpiece *The Pottery Gazette and Glass Trade Review*, whose correspondent wrote on 1 April 1929:

The Bridge Pottery. Beauworth, Alresford, Hants, showed samples of a type of studio pottery which, whilst capable, no doubt, of interesting collectors of novelties, is not entirely designed or intended to compete with the commercially produced article. One could not help thinking that this particular exhibit was one which would probably have had a more homely setting in the Ideal Home Exhibition at Olympia, than in a strictly competitive trade fair such as that at the White City.

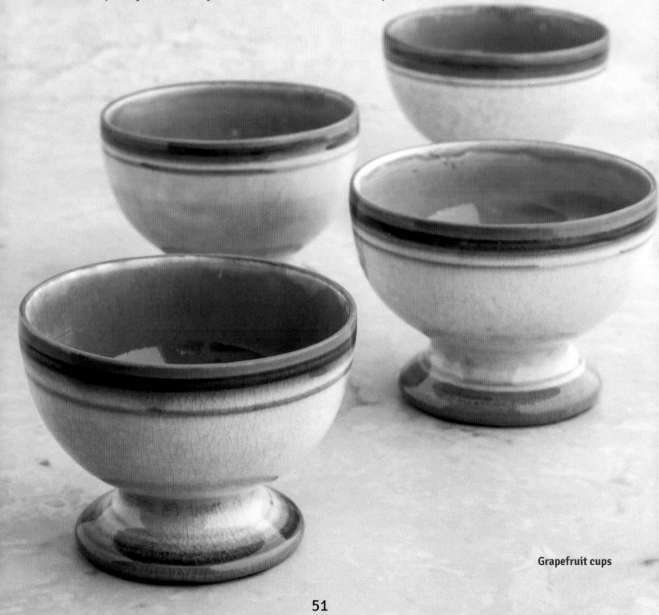

Grapefruit cups

51

The fair had been the wrong forum for her work and she did not exhibit at it again. Eighteen months later a much more favorable impression was given of Dorothy's achievements in Jennifer's 'From My Notebook' column in *The Daily Mirror*. Here Dorothy and her sisters' creativity was recognised and praised in considerably more generous and appealing ways. The article championed Dorothy in her studio pottery niche and possibly marked the high-water of her time in Beauworth.

FROM MY NOTEBOOK *by Jennifer*
The three sisters *Some Extracts*

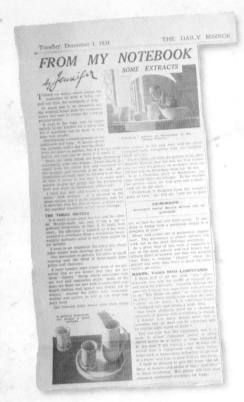

▲ **Extract from Jennifer's Notebook,**
The Daily Mirror, **1 December 1931**

I went to an exhibition the other day where three sisters were showing their work.

One specialises in pottery, the other in hand weaving and the third in home-made jams, jellies and chutneys.

A large London store stocks some of the preserves and so one knows that they are not those "chancy" things which sometimes turn out well and sometimes don't. Some of the jams are those not met with in every store cupboard - bullace and quince and cherry, for instance. Among the jellies were crab apple, medlar and quince, as well as the more ordinary ones.

The weaving sister makes the most attractive scarves in silk and wool, and the prices compare quite favourably with the machine-made articles.

I had a little talk with the pottery sister, Miss Dorothy Watson, and she told me that visitors can see over the pottery on weekdays from ten till five and on Saturdays from ten till one.

It is in a charming place in Hampshire, she says – really three old cottages. In fine weather, the potters – there are four girls and a man – can work in the open.

"Everything is designed from the woman's point of view," she told me, "and are in daily use, so that we can test their utility. If anything is wrong with a particular design it is scrapped at once."

Shape and colour are of paramount importance. The decoration is almost entirely line work, but in the most delicious colourings.

A great deal of this work is supplied to one of the most artistic and best known furnishing firms in London, you may rest assured that there is nothing "chancy" about the pottery any more than there is about the other sister's preserves.

I liked best of all the little "sets" - hors d'eouvres sets and the soufflé or custard sets and those for lemonade. Glancing through the price list I found that some items were referred to as "five dishes on ashet" or "seven pieces on ashet." I have rarely come across the word "ashet" in the South. It is sometimes heard in Scotland still and means a large dish.

One could gradually build-up a charming collection of pottery with everything to match....

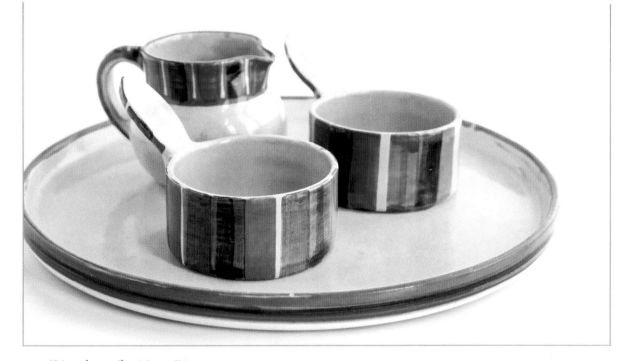

▲ Soufflé set (part of), with small jug

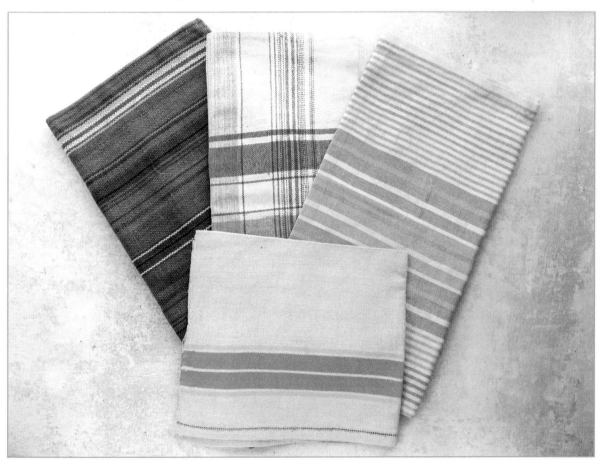

▲ Hand-woven cloth by Ethel Watson

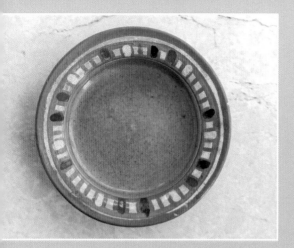

▲ Breakfast plate

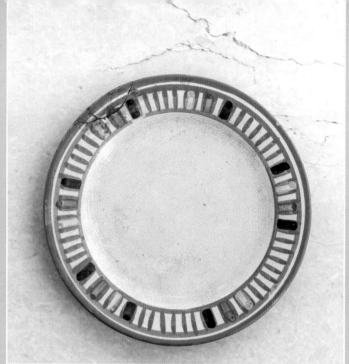

▲ Dinner plate

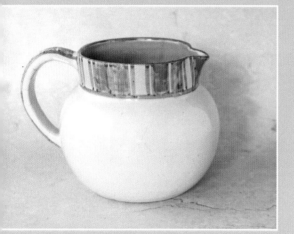

▲ Water or milk jug

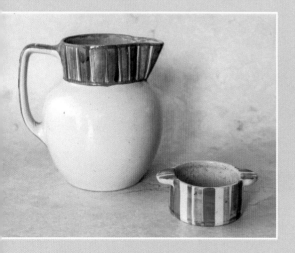

▲ Water or milk jug with egg dish

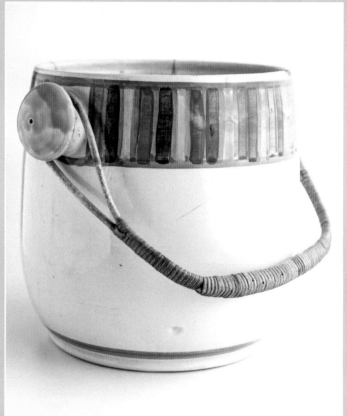

▲ Slop bucket with wicker handle

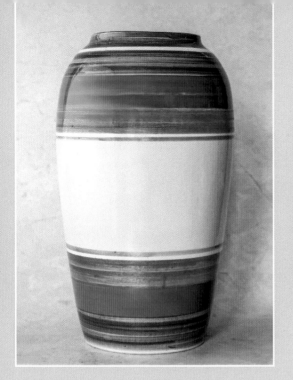

▲ Flower vase, tall

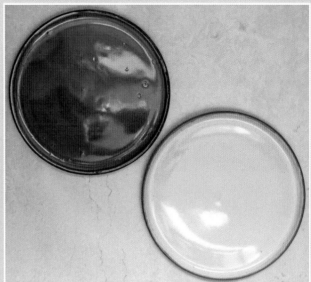

▲ Trays

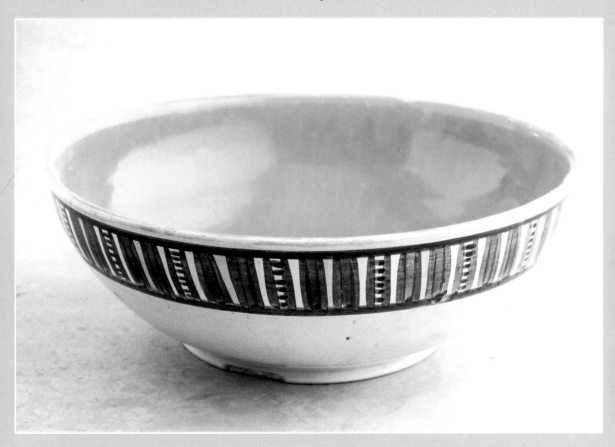

▲ Fruit or salad bowl

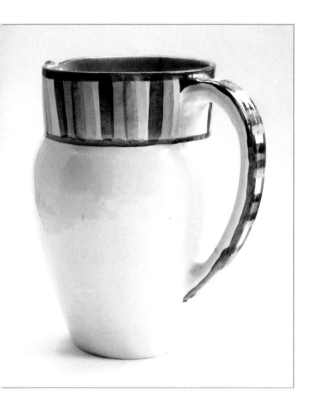

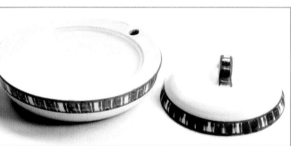

Although the well-to-do home counties were cushioned from the worst effects of the 1930s slump, and Dorothy had the benefit of making wares likely to be sought by those least affected, conditions were poor. Geoffrey Watson recalled the hardships of somebody who helped her: 'A man used to come to look at my aunt's car, and sometimes drive it. He had six sons who used to bicycle many miles in search of work.' Unemployment benefit was minimal and to lose a job left workers at the real risk of absolute poverty.

Dora Lunn's Ravenscourt Pottery and Majel Davidson's at Gushetneuk had already closed by this time but Dorothy struggled on. She had to. She was a stayer with no other way of supporting herself. Nonetheless, by the summer of 1934 she must have been exhausted from working flat-out, seven days a week with all the anxieties, responsibilities and expenses. She decided to give up. By then her cottages and equipment needed complete renewal. Her arrangement to supply Heal's may also have been a contributory factor, for if Dorothy had been unable to keep up with the volume desired, they would likely have turned to larger studio potteries or manufacturers. They probably did. There is a report a few years later of their buyer visiting another small pottery: 'A dapper little man, swaggering about the place making demands and placing sole suppliers under great pressure, with nothing committed to paper'.

Dorothy had had enough; she was exhausted by the struggle. She recalled:

> After ten years of unbelievably hard work (which had its very sunny side), I had had enough of it and sold my lovely cottages. But for innumerable kindnesses of relations and friends we could not have survived.

She is unlikely to have foreseen that her decision would save The Bridge Pottery and most probably her health, and that it was a prudent move. Her goods were placed in store with friends in Devon before Wentways was sold on 16 February 1935, thus ending The Bridge Pottery era at Beauworth. Many years later a subsequent owner of Wentways discovered that Dorothy had appeared to live exclusively on corned

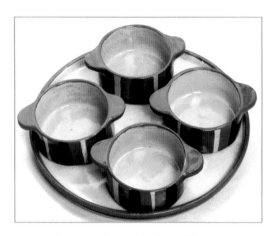

▲ **Large jug, warming dish and soufflé set**

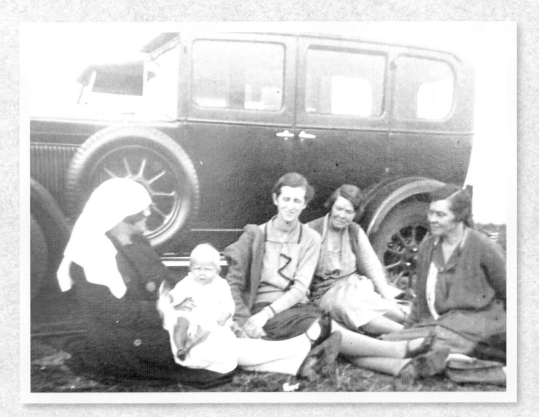

▸ Dorothy (centre right) with Ethel (right) and family group at Beauworth, in front of the Austin 10 car, 1931

▾ A summer picnic, 1934. Grace (left), Dorothy and niece Monica

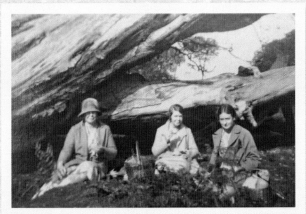

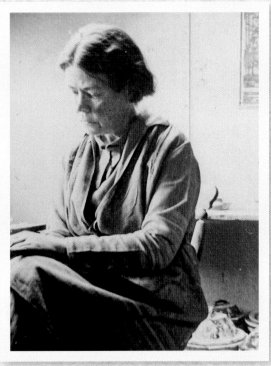

beef, judging from the number of tins unearthed in the rubbish heap.

Dorothy wrote that having closed her pottery in late 1934, she moved to western Somerset, but it is not known exactly where or why. She may have thought to join forces with another pottery. However, given that she used the single word 'fiasco' to describe this move, it would seem to have been short-lived.

▴ A pensive Dorothy, c. 1933

57

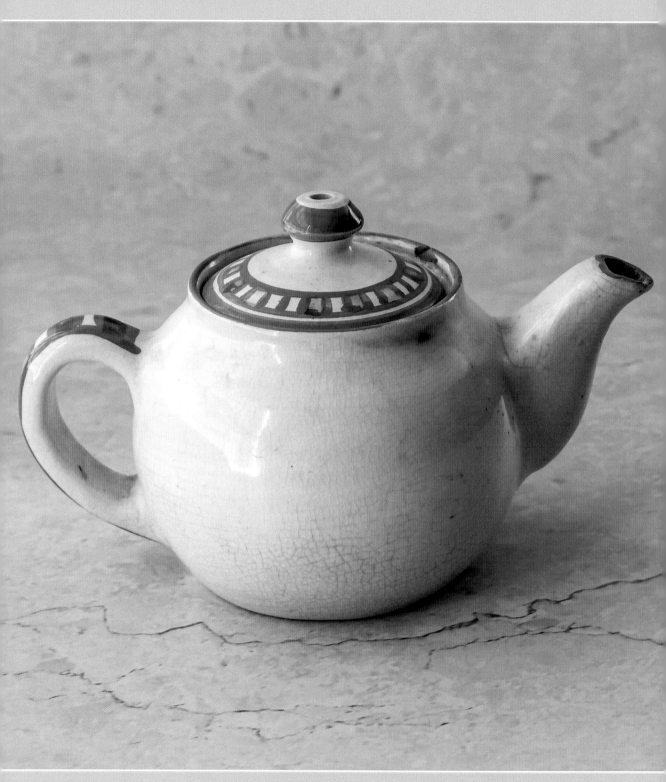

▲ Teapot

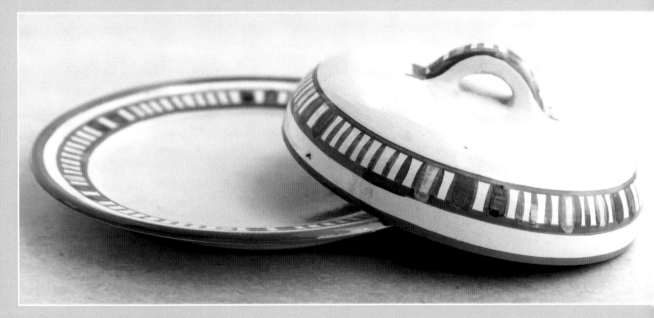

▲ Crumpet dish and lid from breakfast set

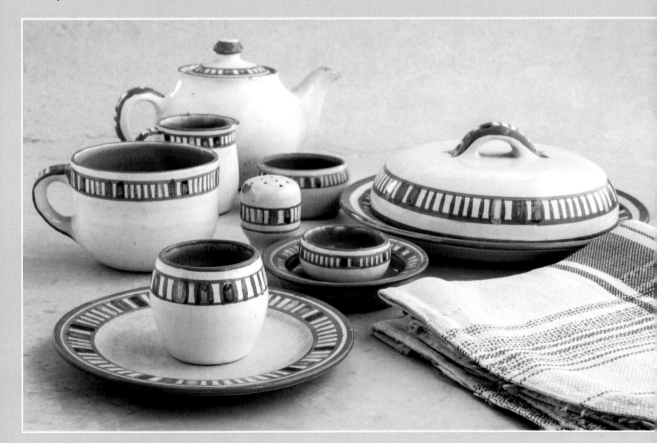

▲ Breakfast set, with hand-woven cloth

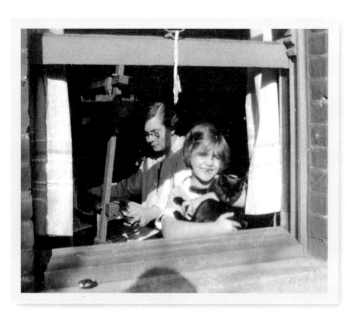

▲ Ethel on her loom, with Ursula and George the cat
at 3 England's Lane, c. 1930

Correspondence reveals that Dorothy was soon living with her mother and Ethel at 3 England's Lane in Hampstead which was a large family house they had taken on in 1927.

Although relieved of the ten-year struggle, the loss of everything she had created at Beauworth must have been bewildering. Nonetheless, that is how events unfolded for Dorothy and at the age of forty six, she was back living with a parent, away from everything she had achieved, and no doubt having lost some of her self-purpose and standing.

Whilst Dorothy had chosen to work in the field of pottery, Ethel had pursued an artistic career becoming Art Mistress at St Christopher's Preparatory School for Girls in Beckenham. She had five pictures hung at The Royal Academy between 1917 and 1921. She was a 'workhorse', looking after Geoffrey, Ursula and her mother, in addition to her teaching job and weaving to sell in conjunction with the pottery. She underpinned the family and so it was natural that in Dorothy's time of uncertainty she should go to England's Lane.

Dorothy recalled that after taking some months to recover, she was on the lookout for suitable premises to set up the pottery again. Unsurprisingly, given her determination, she did not let this ambition rest. Most likely she shared Dora Lunn's philosophy that 'an idealist always follows the gleam of an idea, regardless of incongruity in the lack of worldly possessions'. She had not been put off by her experiences.

Through the good fortune of staying with her younger sister, Grace, in the summer of 1935, Dorothy came across an opportunity to set up her business again. She had much in common with Grace who, after working as a kindergarten teacher, was busy running 'Woodland Preserves', her jam-making enterprise. In a similar way to Dorothy's arrangement with Heal's, she supplied exclusive London stores including Fortnum & Mason in Piccadilly. Grace ran her business from Rectory Cottage, Little Horsted, near Uckfield in East Sussex where she had also set up a tea-room.

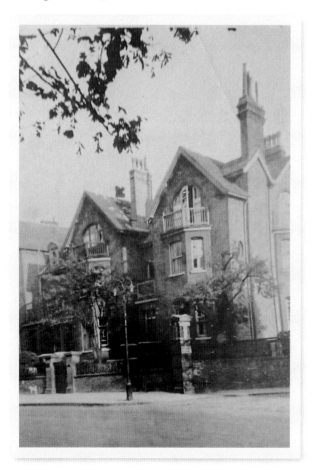

◄ 3 England's Lane, Hampstead, London in 1933

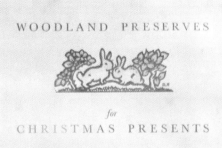

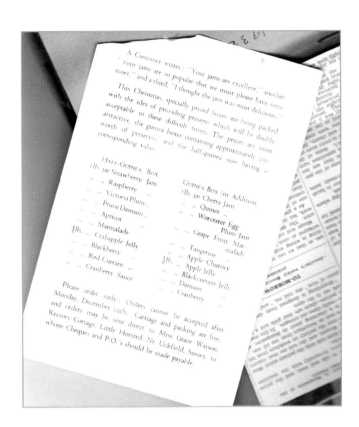

▲ ▶ **Woodland Preserves Christmas list, 1932**

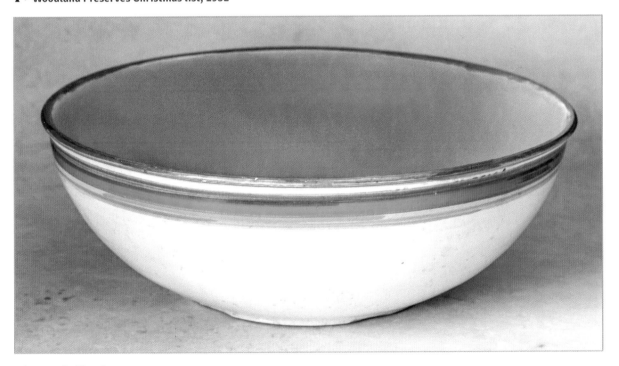

▲ **Large salad bowl**

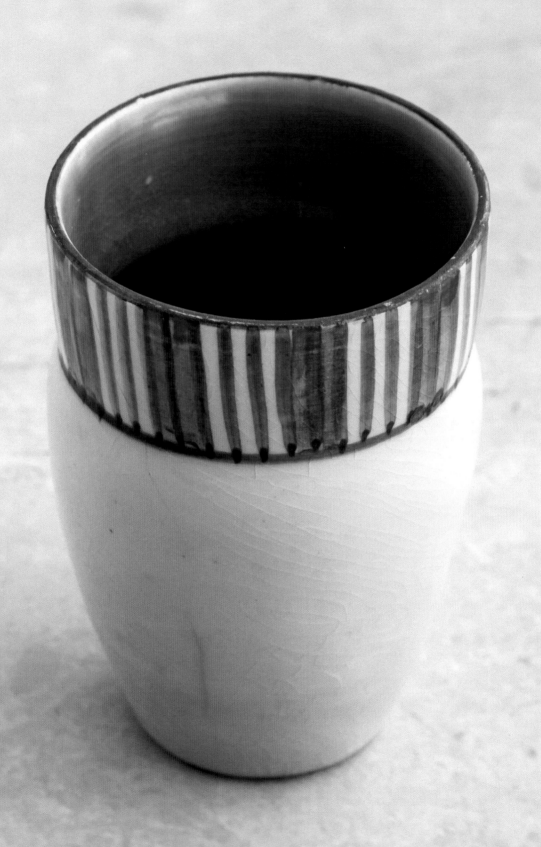

CHAPTER 5

Lime House, Rolvenden

n June 1935, by which time she was aged forty seven, Dorothy spotted Lime House and its adjoining buildings in the mid-Kent village of Rolvenden, near Cranbrook. She and Ethel had been staying with Grace near Uckfield and were actively looking for a suitable property. Their search had taken them over to Pevensey the day before and Ethel noted in her diary for 17-20 June, 'three days pottery hunting with D. Very cold and wet. Found a cottage with sheds at Rolvenden which may do'. Dorothy wrote:

It took me a year to recover from the Beauworth Pottery venture, and then I started to look for premises more suited to my advancing years. A long search ended in Rolvenden where I arrived in 1935, nearly penniless but happy, because I had found what I wanted.

Lime House, which had been unoccupied for over a year, was available unfurnished. The semi-detached house offered a drawing and living room, kitchen and scullery, two principal bedrooms and two smaller bedrooms. Lime Cottage was attached to the east of the house but was not part of the lease. Notably for Dorothy, the letting particulars also described:

Adjoining the house to the West is a long range of outbuildings built partly of brick and tiles and of timber and corrugated iron, all in very good repair. The near building is about 25' long by 16' deep with double door opening onto the road; adjoining and communicating is another portion about 15' square, and beyond this the larger portion about 32' 6" long and 15' 6" deep, also with double hung entrance door opening onto the road. These building[s] are bare of any fittings or appliances and would be extremely useful for many purposes.

◄ **Cider cup**

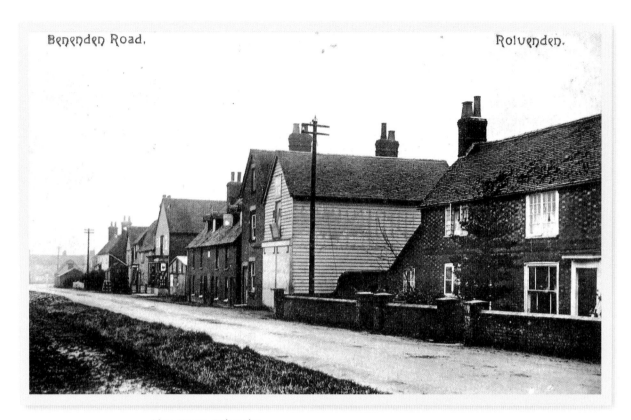

Benenden Road.   Rolvenden.

▲ Lime House, Rolvenden

Dorothy wrote straightaway on 20 June, to enquire:

> *If I went there it would be to carry on my business of Art Pottery maker and I should want to use the sheds as workshops and showroom. I should be grateful if you would enquire from the Landlord: 1) Whether there would be any objection to this business. 2) Whether he would be prepared to put the sheds into repair for this purpose... floors, walls, roof and more natural light.*

Colonel Arthur Barham of Hole Park responded the same day confirming that the answers were affirmative. They arranged to meet a week later, and he wrote to her again on 5 July to send builders specifications for the adaptation of the outbuilding into a pottery and the creation of a showroom. With enthusiasm, Colonel Barham added ' …I think the showroom will come out very well with an old-fashioned shop window'. Enlivened by the prospect of re-founding her pottery, Dorothy replied to Colonel Barham, 'I think it is satisfactory in every detail and I should be glad if the work could be done as soon as possible. What is the earliest date that I can have possession of the cottage and how soon can the repairs to the sheds be finished?'

Work started straightaway to lay new floors, open up partition walls and improve

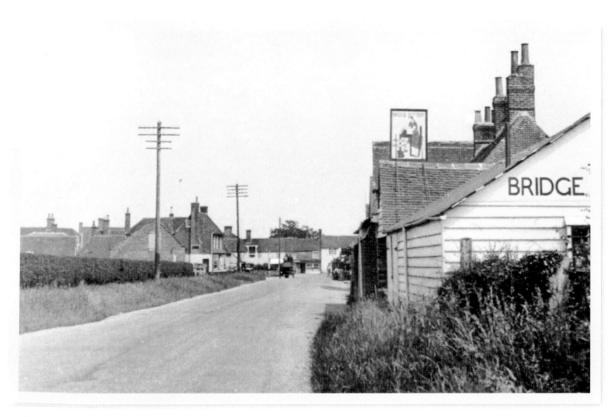

▲ The Bridge Pottery, Rolvenden, 1936, from Benenden Road

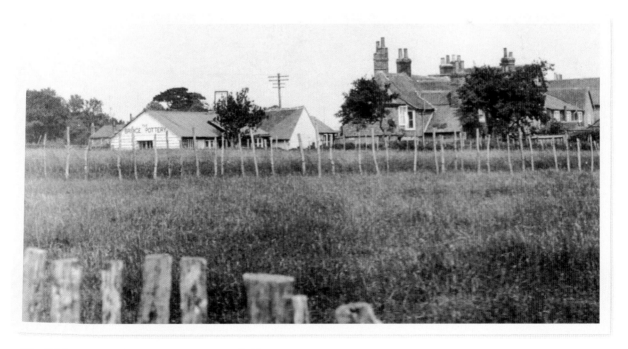

▲ The Bridge Pottery from the south-western field

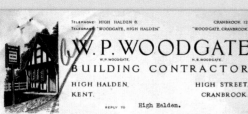

TELEPHONE: HIGH HALDEN 8. CRANBROOK 12.
TELEGRAMS: "WOODGATE, HIGH HALDEN" "WOODGATE, CRANBROOK"

W. P. WOODGATE
W. P. WOODGATE H. B. WOODGATE
BUILDING CONTRACTOR

HIGH HALDEN, HIGH STREET,
KENT. CRANBROOK.

REPLY TO High Halden.

FS.

Specification and Estimate. July 4th, 1935.

Col. A. S. Barham.,
Hole Park,
Rolvenden, Kent.

Dear Sir, re. Lime House, Rolvenden - Buildings.

We thank you for your kind enquiry and have much
pleasure in quoting you as under:-

Shed with Slated Roof. Excavate over floor to an approximate
depth of 6", level and fill up existing pit with earth from
excavations; lay 4" Portland Cement concrete over floor,
fix 3" x 2" splayed deal fillets as joists at about 1' 6" centres
and fill in between with fine breeze concrete; cover last with
1" square edge flooring creosoted on underside. Fix small fillet
at intersection of floor with walls. - Line the studding, including
gables, with flat asbestos sheeting. Take off sloping weatherboard
to front of shed; fix glazing bars at 1' 6" centres and glaze with
21 Oz clear sheet glass; Take out the four fixed sashes at rear
of shed and adapt to open, hung on steel butt hinges and fitted
with casement stays and fasteners; repair the door and frame
leading to garden and repair the weatherboard in places as necessary;
Lime-white on the brick walls and asbestos sheeting.

(NOTE: - The rafters still to be left exposed).

Shed with Tile Roof.

Strip the tiles and battens from roof; re-batten
with 1" x 3/4" battens and re-lay tiles, making out with new tiles
as necessary; Fix new gutter bearers and boarding where this
roof adjoins slated roof and form new 4 lb lead gutter; remove
the door and frame from front of building also take down the one
brick wall and quoin up; pull down old partition inside shed and
clear away; excavate over floor a depth as required and lay 4" Portland
Cement Concrete; on last from front of building to a depth of 6ft
x full width lay 9" x 9" Red quarry tiles. (No skirting), render
the remainder of the floor smooth in cement and sand; board up
doorway leading to No. 3. shed; line the underside of rafters
with "Treetex" ceiling board and twice whiten. Clean and point
walls as necessary and limewhite;
Form concrete channel in front of entrance to carry water into
gulley in ditch.

- 1 -

W. P. WOODGATE. CONTINUATION SHEET No. 1.

July 4th 1935.

To Col. A. S. Barham.,

Shop Front. Form shop front 6ft back from entrance of half
brick base wall 2' 0" high off floor level, using the bricks from
pulling down; render on brickwork internally; fix 6" x 3"
wrot deal sill with 4" x 2½" window frame; fix in centre 4" x 3"
rebated door frame for door 6' 3" high x 2' 6" wide; fix 1½"
glazing bars to window forming 12 squares on either side of
door each approx. 15" high and 14" wide; glaze window in 21 Oz
clear sheet glass; provide and fix door 1½" thick with panel at
bottom, the upper half of door to be glazed as windows. Fix
lock and furniture to door, p. c. 6/-d set. Fill in gable above
window with 3" x 2" studding covered one side only with 3/4"
V jointed matchboard.

NO PAINTING ALLOWED FOR.

To carry out the foregoing works, would cost:-

Approximately .. £85. 0. 0.

We hope to be favoured with your kind instructions
which will have our careful attention.

Yours faithfully,

W P Woodgate
B.

---

*Primrose
4222.*

*3 Englands Lane
Hampstead
N.W.3.
17/7/35. recd 22-7-35*

*The Barham Estates Ltd.
Dear Sirs,*

*If Colonel Barham is
willing to accept me as a
tenant for Lime House, Rolvenden,
I should be much obliged if a date
(as early as possible) could be fixed
for possession. I want to make
arrangements for my goods to be
fetched from Devonshire. Would
it be possible to ring me up on
this subject, as it is very urgent?*

*Yours ffly
Dorothy Watson P.T.O.*

▲ **One of Dorothy's letters to Colonel Barham about lease arrangements for her new pottery at Lime House, Rolvenden, 17 July 1935, before moving in**

◄ **Specification and estimate by W. P. Woodgate, Building Contractors, 4 July 1935**

the windows and ventilation. The new shopfront was constructed six feet back from the pavement line and the tin roof was painted red to look like roofing tiles.

Dr T. V. Good from Regent's Park in London wrote to confirm, 'Miss Watson is quite reliable and satisfactory, not very well off but I should describe her as financially sound.' From the Chichester Cathedral Deanery, Mrs Catherine M. Duncan-Jones, Dorothy's old schoolfriend and rival from Cambridge, confirmed that she had 'known Miss Dorothy Watson for most of her life and should consider her in every way a desirable tenant,

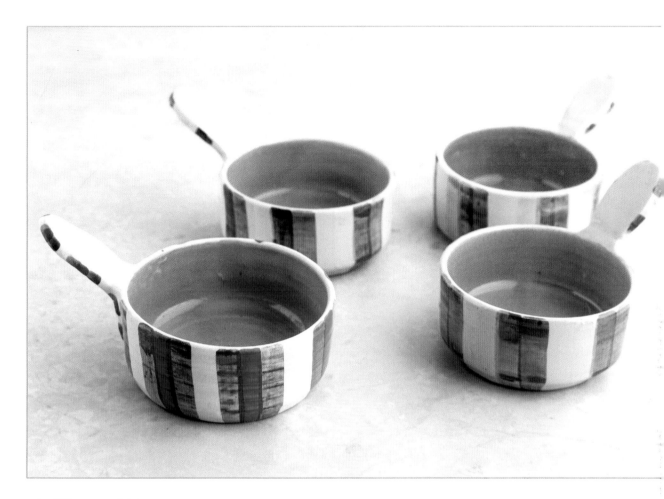

▲ Soufflé or custard dishes

both careful & entirely trustworthy'. Work proceeded quickly and by 27 July, after adjustments to the pottery had been made so that electric kilns could be brought in from the road front, the lease was agreed. Dorothy wrote: 'Thank you for speeding up matters. I am arranging for my furniture to arrive before the end of next week and should like to take possession.'

On 2 August 1935, Dorothy signed the lease for an initial fourteen years at a rent of £54 per annum and she moved into the Lime House on the same day. After a flurry of activity, driven as much by Dorothy's determination and excitement at re-establishing her pottery as it was by Colonel Barham's desire to see her move in, The Bridge Pottery had been reborn. Arthur, who had helped to build and install equipment in her previous two potteries, came with his son Stephen to help set things up.

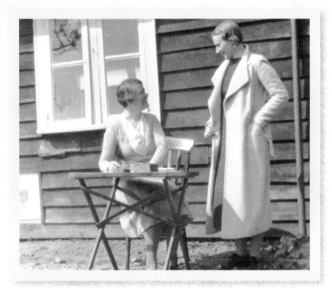

▲ Dorothy, seated, with
Miss Whitehouse, May 1936

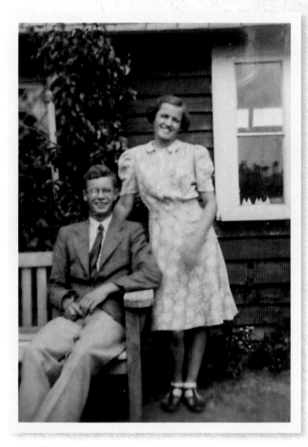

▲ Geoffrey and Ursula at the pottery

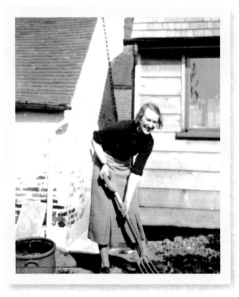

▲ Miss Whitehouse gardening
outside Ethel's new weaving
shed, 1936

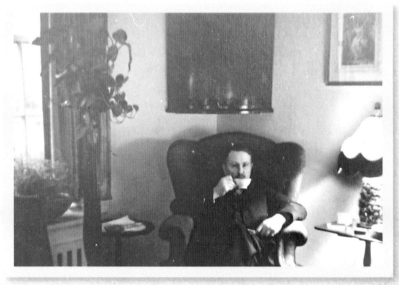

▲ Frederick Watson on his last visit to Lime House, October 1938

Dorothy later wrote about her new arrangement: 'The small house and roomy workshop combine the maximum convenience with the minimum of labour'. She installed two pottery wheels, two kilns and wooden turntables to facilitate hand painting. At last, with running water, electric heating and lighting and electric kilns she had a 'non-labour' set-up to match Majel Davidson's Gushetneuk Pottery, all be it in rather spartan converted sheds.

Dorothy was helped by Miss Whitehouse and Betty Stanard from the village and she soon began to produce her wares. She worked hard to re-establish the pottery. Filling her showroom and finding local shops who would stock her wares was the priority. One of her regular customers was Mr Charles Danks who ran Harlequin, a 'super' gift shop and modern art gallery close to the seafront at Bexhill in East Sussex. With the public's keen interest in the town's striking art deco De La Warr Pavilion which was completed on the seafront in 1935, this was a popular resort. Dorothy also supplied shops and galleries further away such as The Oak Gallery in Leamington Spa which had sold her wares before. It was again advertising The Bridge Pottery in October 1935.

Dorothy also revived her pattern of attending local fairs and shows, even going as far as Berkshire to pick up where she had left off in 1934. *The Times* reported on her stall at The Royal Counties Show in Reading on 5 June 1937: '…exhibits of the produce of rural industries are always popular. … A large selection of handcrafts is always exhibited in the arts and crafts pavilion. New designs of Bridge Pottery include what is described as the perfect jam jar, which is so formed as to prevent the entrance of dust or wasps.'

In the summer of 1936, Dorothy was joined in Rolvenden by her mother, then aged seventy nine, and Ethel with Geoffrey and Ursula who were then aged sixteen and thirteen. Ethel recorded in her diary: '1936 A year of change for the family. On July 8, mother and I with G & U left England's Lane, Hampstead, which we have let and came to live with D at Rolvenden'.

The children didn't stay long as that summer

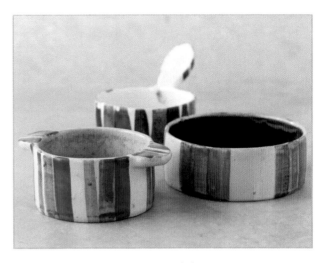

▲ **Soufflé or custard dish with egg dishes**

Geoffrey left Christ's Hospital School and set off for his first working adventure in South America. In September, Ursula left for Abbots Bromley School in Staffordshire, where she had won a scholarship. When she was home for the holidays, Colonel Barham's grandchildren Ruth, Daphne and David remember being invited to the pottery for dancing parties with her. Earlier in 1936, Margaret had returned from Grahamstown on leave and stayed until October.

Ethel initially moved her weaving looms into a garden shed behind the house. She wrote to Colonel Barham on 3 September 1936 about erecting a new more substantial building behind the pottery which she would pay for herself. With his agreement, her new prefabricated timber 'Colt House' was put up with gas, electricity and water laid on. The sisters' great nephew, Paul Watson, believes that Ethel's weaving was always on a small scale and that she made place mats, sofa cushion covers and the like. She must have been delighted to get her enterprise properly established and housed, alongside the pottery.

Dorothy made smaller items in Rolvenden than she had at Wentways and developed simpler decorative patterns, such as incorporating green and grey stripes. Her ivory-toned clay continued to come from Fulham Pottery,

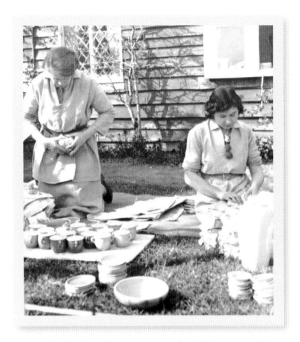 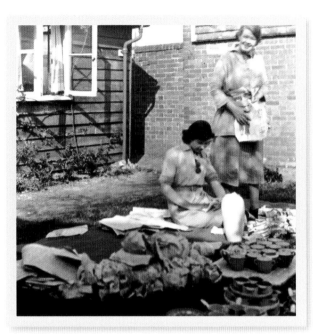

▲ Dorothy, left, with Betty Stanard packing pottery in newspaper for shipment, 1936

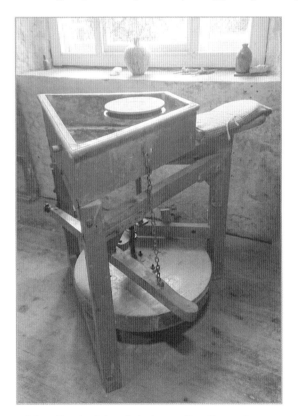

▲ A treadle wheel, Leach design, as Dorothy used

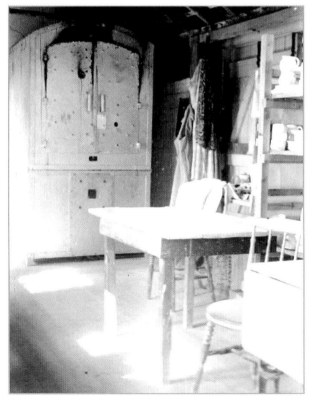

▲ Electric kiln at The Bridge Pottery, 1936, with overheating damage to kiln doors and roof timbers

and she continued to throw using treadle wheels, as before.
From Ethel's photograph of one of the electric kilns in 1936, a type
manufactured for smaller scale commercial users, it seems to have
been obtained well-used. Buckled doors and blackened roof timbers
indicate that despite all the conveniences of her new arrangement,
in comparison to Wentways, she still faced difficulties and fire risks.

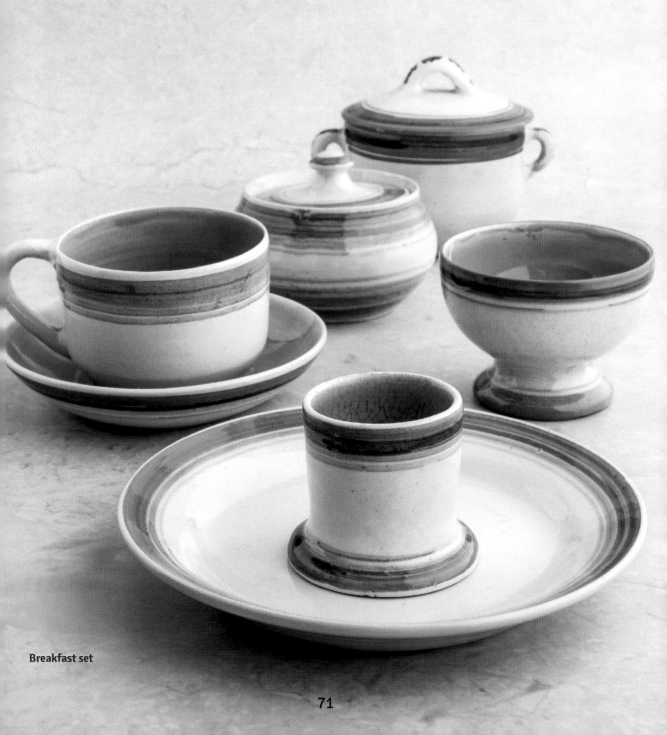

Breakfast set

The Coronation of King George VI and Queen Elizabeth on 12 May 1937 was well celebrated in Rolvenden. Dorothy decorated her roadside frontage with bunting and flags and dressed up with her assistants as ancient Syrian potters. She gave pottery demonstrations and sold Coronation souvenirs for 1/-. She also produced small commemorative pots.

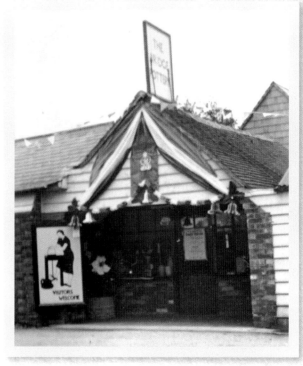

▶ Advertisement in Rolvenden village souvenir pamphlet for the Coronation

▲ Pottery showroom dressed for the Coronation, 12 May 1937

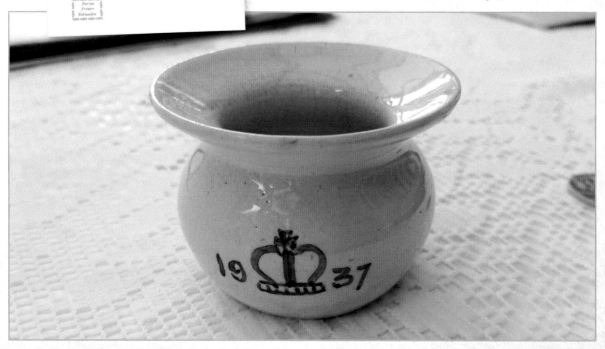

▲ Coronation vase 1937

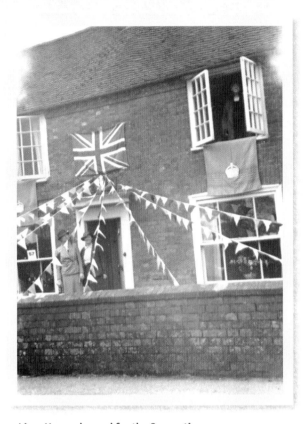

▲ Lime House dressed for the Coronation

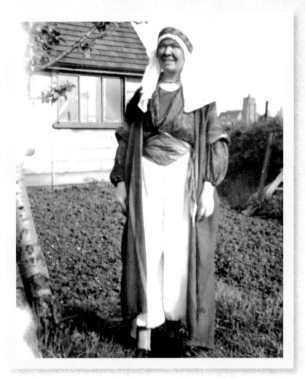

▲ Dorothy outside the new weaving shed, dressed as an 'ancient' potter in a blue shirt, white trousers, red sash, and green, yellow and orange cloak

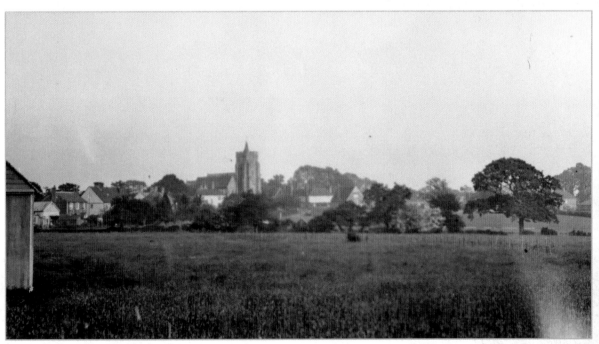

▲ View from south of the pottery towards Rolvenden Church c. 1937

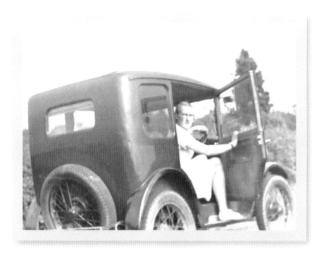

▲ Miss Whitehouse in her Austin 7 'Widoor'
[wide door] fabric bodied model, circa 1937.
The car was first registered in 1929

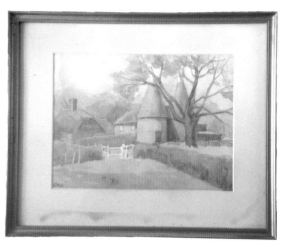

▲ Ethel's watercolour of Windmill Farm,
opposite the pottery

Alongside the pottery, Ethel continued to
produce her bold woven fabrics and she found time
to paint local scenes. She imaginatively captured
the local landscape for her photo album, getting
about with Miss Whitehouse in an Austin Seven
'wide-door' car.

In November 1937, Bridge pottery was on display
at the Applied Arts and Handicrafts Exhibition at
the Royal Horticultural Hall in Westminster. Again,
a reporter from *The Times* commented: 'There is
something, too, to be said for The Bridge Pottery'.
The following year the *Kent & Sussex Courier*
carried an account on 22 July of The Bridge Pottery
stall at the Five Villages Fair at Withyham, Sussex:
'Some pretty examples of Kentish pottery, The
Bridge Pottery at Rolvenden giving a demonstration
of the whole process from raw clay to the finished
article.' On 21 July 1939, the *Courier* again reported
on The Bridge Pottery's display at the Tunbridge
Wells and South-Eastern Counties Agricultural
Show: 'Some of the items came from Bridge
Potteries at Rolvenden, where jars and vases,
designed on the premises, are thrown on the wheel,
hand painted and glazed, moulds being rarely used.'

And so the pattern for Dorothy went on for four
years after she arrived in Rolvenden. After a lot of
hard work, and with the close support of Ethel as
well as her helpers from the village, Dorothy had the
pottery well established again, but she was not to

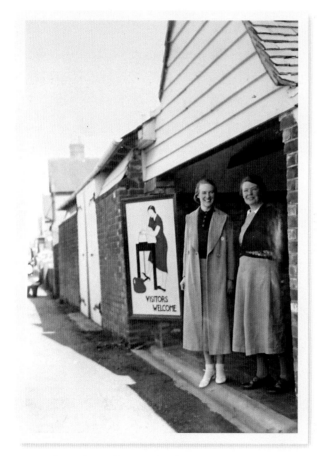

▲ Dorothy, right, with Miss Whitehouse,
outside the pottery, 1937, with the Austin 7
behind, parked on the pavement

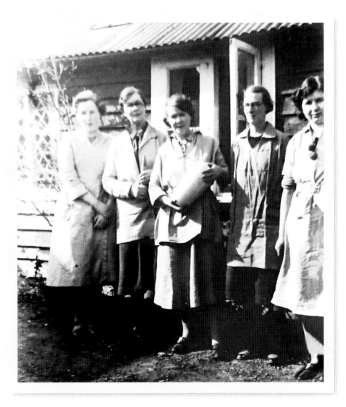

have known that these newspaper reports were some of the last compliments to her success.

Ethel's diary records her increasing anxiety about menacing events on the Continent during the summer of 1939. She recorded that on 8 July the village received its first taste of what was to come with a civil defence drill:

Tonight, there has been a blackout and a bomb was supposed to fall on the pottery, D having been warned that it was coming. A troop of youths and maidens came along to be casualties and then members of the ambulance crew came along and tended them and took them off to the Voluntary Aid Detachment hut where they had further treatment. There were two shell shocked ones, D being one of them and these caused amusement during the evening.

▲ Dorothy (centre), with Ethel (second left), Gwynath Goddard (far left), Miss Whitehouse (second right) and Betty Stanard (far right), by the new pottery in Rolvenden, 1939, with names recorded by Mrs Hook in the Rolvenden WI scrapbook, 1939

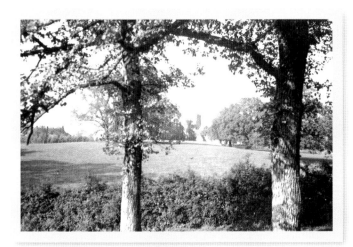

▲ 'Oak brows' form a Bridge mark framing a view of St Mary's Church, Rolvenden, from the south-east, c. 1937

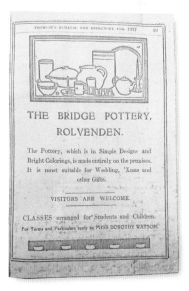

▲ Whole page advertisement in *Thomson Almanac and Directory* 1937, published by W Thomson, High Street, Tenterden, from Mrs Hook's scrapbook

75

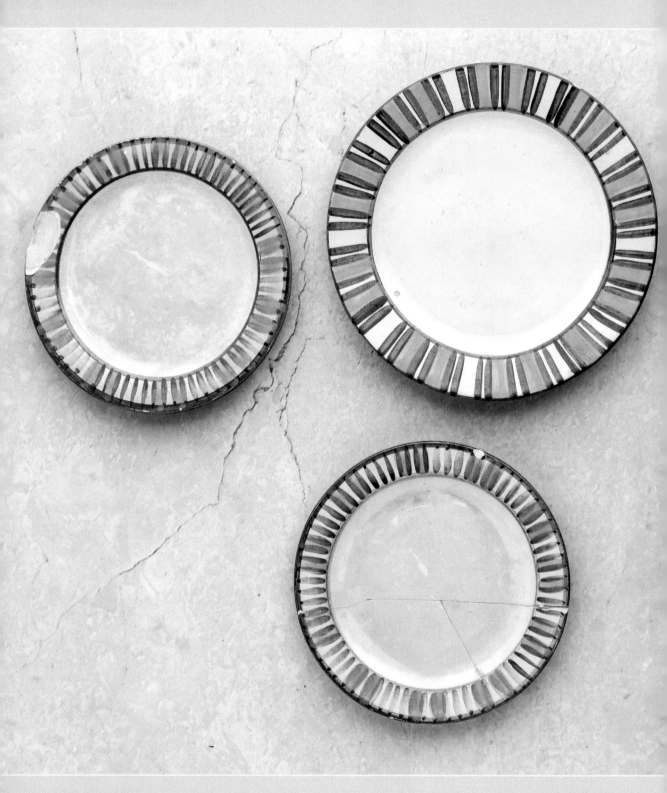

▲ **Tea service plates**

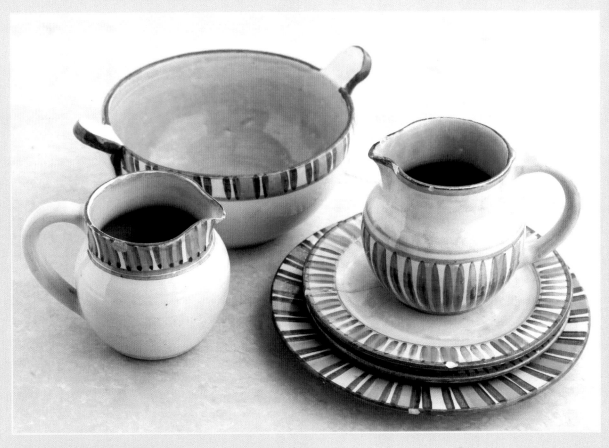

▲ **Plates, jugs and porringer**

On 25 July, Ursula set off for Dieppe in France for three weeks to improve her French. Anxieties had grown sufficiently by the time she returned that Dorothy hesitated about going to the Three Counties Show in Hereford, in case war was declared and she was unable to get back. The start of Ursula's school term was delayed. Earlier in the summer, Gwynath Goddard, who had just left school, had been taken on. She had to be laid off after just six weeks when it looked as though the pottery would have to close.

Dorothy recorded that the pottery was not in production during the war. Fuel and materials would not have been available for a non-essential enterprise and the pottery's closure brought to an end the brief years of optimism for Dorothy and Ethel, as they created their pottery and weaving ideals. For the village register made on the eve of war, Ethel and her mother Margaret Lockhart were listed as living with

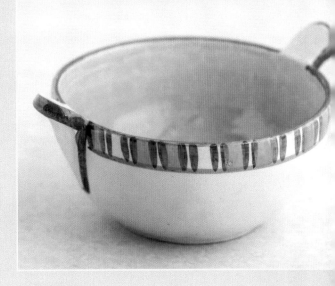

▲ **Porringer**

77

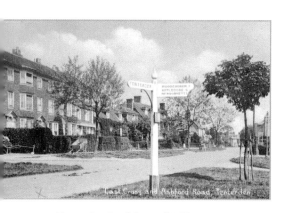

▲ Tenterden Food Control Office was at
No. 9 East Cross, second door on left

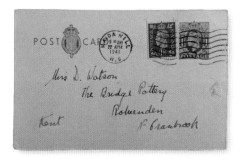

▲ Post card from Grace in London dated
22 April 1941, giving details of the Blitz

Dorothy at Lime House. Dorothy's name had been
put down for important work in the Ministry of Food,
helping to oversee local storage and distribution at the
Food Control Office in Tenterden.

On 19 March 1940, Arthur, who had helped to set up
Dorothy's potteries, died aged fifty seven whilst living at
his Rectory in Ufford, near Stamford, Lincolnshire. He had
married Olive, who had come to stay at the family home
in Cambridge after their father's death in 1906, and the
couple went on to have ten children.

Grace had moved to Minster-in-Thanet in 1936 to run
The Old Oak Guest House. The town changed from 1937
when it became a designated centre for German refugees
and her guest house was most likely requisitioned. She
moved to London and by the advent of war, was Chef at
Westminster Hospital. She lived in Chiswick and shared
with Dorothy by post card several of her experiences
during the Blitz.

In Rolvenden, Dorothy and Ethel shared responsibility
for looking after their elderly mother, who by this time
was infirm and very deaf. They had also taken in another
invalid lady and her companion to live in one of the
pottery flatlets. Ethel recorded in her dairy that 'Mother
had not been quite up to the mark' and on 30 May 1942,
Margaret Lockhart died at Lime House, aged eighty five.
With circumstances making it impractical for her to be
interred with Frederick in Cambridge, her funeral took
place at St Mary's Church, Rolvenden, and she was buried
in the churchyard where her grave was marked with
a simple oak cross. She left effects to the value of
£1,634 15s 2d.

The passing of Dorothy's mother was the start of several
changes at Lime House. The first person to go was Ursula
in the summer of 1942, who having left boarding school in
Staffordshire, excitedly went off to join the Women's Royal
Naval Service at their training depot in Mill Hill, north
London. Next, on 20 June, Ethel returned to London to
take up a secretarial position in a war savings society. She
lived with Grace at 9 Clifton Gardens, Chiswick, leaving
Dorothy in Rolvenden on her own.

For both Ethel and Grace, Rolvenden provided respite
whenever they could get leave and they would travel down
to Tenterden by train. Ethel recorded bridge parties in the
pottery and going out picnicking. In January 1943, she
recorded intense military activity and German bombing
raids with several houses destroyed one night in nearby
High Halden. Dorothy didn't hear the air raid and slept

right through. Without the need for her four-bedroomed house, Dorothy moved into the western end of the pottery which she had previously converted as a flatlet where there was a basic kitchen, bedroom and sitting room. She was to live there for the rest of her time in Rolvenden. This allowed her to sub-let Lime House.

Later in 1943, Christopher, who had served as a schoolmaster, was ordained as a priest in the crypt of St Paul's Cathedral. In 1944, he was appointed Assistant Master and Chaplain at Sutton Valence School about thirteen miles from Rolvenden, and was able to visit Dorothy. Another important family occasion during the bleak war years was nephew Geoffrey's wedding to Kathleen on 6 April 1944.

It is not clear when Dorothy was released from her food control appointment, but she recorded that she got the pottery buildings back from refugees in 1945. Some time after that she was able to turn her attention to setting up The Bridge Pottery once again.

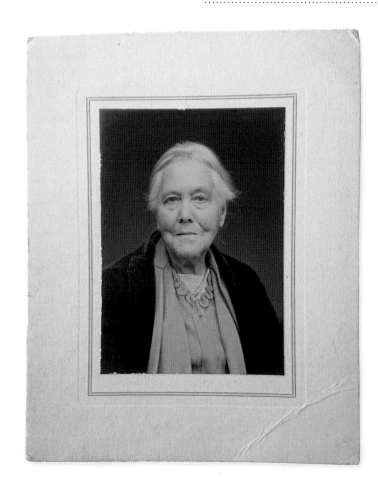

▲ **Margaret Lockhart Watson, aged 83, in 1939**

After the conflict, Dorothy recorded some of her impressions from the beginning of the war onwards.

WHAT THE WAR 1930-1945 HAS MEANT TO ME

We had been living on the edge of a precipice for so long that we began to think that it was almost impossible to topple over into the abyss below. So it was a rather breath-taking experience for me when one of my friends came and told me that he had enlisted in the territorials. This really did look like war, and before many weeks had passed war was indeed declared.

I can only describe my impressions in a series of pictures, and the first of these is of helping Mother to dress on the morning of Sunday, Sept 3, 1939, and getting her settled in her chair preparatory to taking her to church. We had barely got on our way, when we were met by an excited warden who told me that an air raid warning had been sounded. Our instructions were to get off the streets during an air raid, so I turned back, much to Mother's annoyance, whose weekly outing was thus curtailed and who informed me (truly) that she would be quite as safe in church as at home. A few minutes later the church goers returned and told us that the announcement of the beginning of hostilities had been made from the pulpit. It had begun.

It had long been decided that as soon as the war began, I was to go and work for the Food Office in Tenterden, and my instructions were to report at once. Next morning, I reported, but they were not ready for my services, and there was to be a somewhat weary lag of two months. These two months of anticipation were spent by me in preparing two of my workshops as a flatlet which was in fact used by refugees from the coast during all the war years, and has only now (July 1945) come back into my possession; and in canvassing a certain part of the village to find out what accommodation was available for child refugees. My finding on this matter was that where the house was already full to overflowing the extra child was readily welcomed, where there were plenty of empty rooms the welcome was much more lukewarm.

Found my initiation to Food Office Work, at first distressingly light, and later far too heavy. A daily ride into Tenterden and back loomed large as one of the minor discomforts, when fire-watching became the order of the day, as it did quite soon in these coastal districts, one night it was spent in positive discomfort on a hard little camp bed at the office. One was fully dressed and ready to turn out at a moment's notice, but nothing

WHAT THE WAR 1939-1945 HAS MEANT TO ME

We had been living on the edge of a precipice for so long, that we began to think it was almost impossible to topple over into the abyss below, so it was rather a breath-taking experience for me when one of my friends came and told me that he had enlisted in the territorials. This really did look like war, and before many weeks had passed war was indeed declared.

I can only describe my impressions in a series of pictures, and the first of these is of helping Mother to dress on the morning of Sunday, Sept. 3rd, 1939, and getting her settled in her chair preparatory to taking her to church. We had barely got on our way, when we were met by an excited warden, who told me that an air raid warning had been sounded. Our instructions were to get off the streets during an air raid, so I turned back, much to Mother's annoyance, whose weekly outing was thus curtailed and who informed me (truly) that she would be quite as safe in church as at home. A few minutes later the church goers returned and told us that the announcement of the beginning of hostilities had been made from the pulpit. It had begun.

It had long been decided that as soon as the war began I was to go and work in the Food Office in Tenterden, and my instructions were to report at once. Next morning I reported, but they were not ready for my services, and there was to be a somewhat weary lag of two months. These two months of anticipation were spent by me in preparing two of my workshops as a

and the inevitable "have you heard....?" was received by him in dead silence for a moment. His face was chalky white, but in a minute or so he sat down at his table and said with something of a swagger "Well we're in it alone now."

Dunkirk came next - that bitter moment of defeat which was turned into something which closely resembled a glorious victory. The ladies of Kent remembered it particularly because they had the privilege of preparing and distributing food to the train loads of weary men who went through Headcorn station. I wanted to be one of them, but at this moment people from the coastal areas began to be seriously alarmed and to flock into our village and all the villages in this district, and I had to find accommodation for an invalid lady and her companion in this house.

The next picture in my mind is conjured up by the sound of endless heavy bombers

The Battle of Britain was fought over Kent: one might say over Rolvenden, and we remember it as one of the greatest thrills of our life. The sky seemed to be endlessly blue, and day after day, hour after hour, the tiny glittering planes chased each other across the sky, leaving their trail of white in the clouds: airmen bailed out and were seen to float slowly, oh so slowly groundwards, sometimes with a guardian angel in the form of a plane circling round them to protect them, and planes — enemy and our own crashed to right and left of us. On one occasion four of us, including mother who at 94 was very deaf, were having dinner while a battle was in progress. The planes were coming so low that they actually cast a shadow across the table, but in order not to alarm mother we went on with our meal and our chat as if nothing was happening.

The next picture in my mind is conjured up by the sound of endless heavy bombers passing overhead night after night on their way to London. It was a ghastly, deadly drone, and had barely ceased when the returning bombers (which we liked to tell ourselves were fewer in number) came on the scene. Sometimes a single one would circle the house, trying to decide down which chimney to drop its unwanted bombs ...... On one night we saw such a glow in the sky that we knew or thought we knew

actually happened while I was on guard and I can't help feeling I should not have been of much practical use if it had.

A few days leave from the office coincided with the fall of France. Ethel and I had gone to Hastings for the day, and we were sitting having lunch in a restaurant largely frequented by young air-force men. The tragic news was announced on the one o'clock news and a waitress who heard it came and whispered it to a client, who in turn passed it on quietly to a friend. In a very short time, all the lunchers knew and the tension in there was oppressive. Another air-force boy came into the room, and the inevitable "have you heard ....?" was received by him in dead silence for a minute. His face was chalky white, but in a minute or so he sat down at his table and said with something of a swagger, "Well, we're in it alone now."

Dunkirk came next - that bittersweet moment of defeat which was turned into something which closely resembled glorious victory. The ladies of Kent remember it particularly because they had the privilege of preparing and distributing food to the train loads of weary men who went through Headcorn station. I wanted to be one of them, but at this moment people from the coastal areas began to be seriously alarmed and to flock into our village and all the villages in this district, and I had to find accommodation for an invalid lady and her companion in this house.

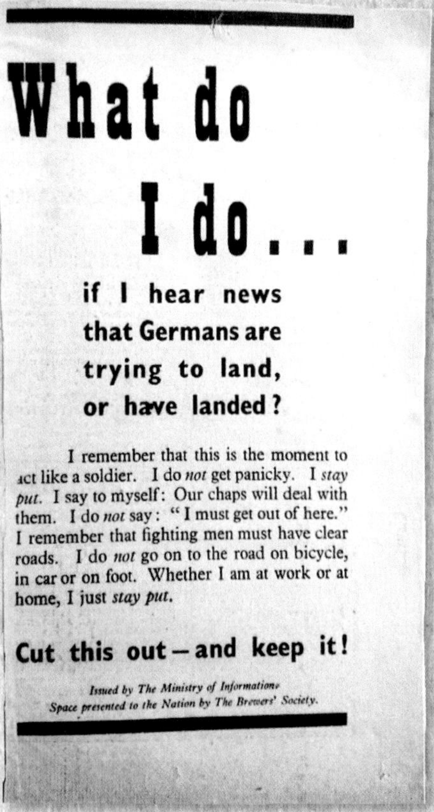

...The Battle of Britain was fought over Kent: one might say over Rolvenden, and we remember it as one of the greatest thrills of our life. The sky seemed to be endlessly blue, day after day, hour after hour, the tiny glittering planes chasing each other across the sky, leaving their trails of white in the clouds: airmen bailed out and were seen to float slowly, oh so slowly, groundwards, sometimes with a guardian angel in the form of a plane circling round them to protect them, and enemy planes and our own crashed to the right and left of us. On one occasion four of us, including Mother, who at 84 was very deaf, were having dinner while a battle was in progress. The planes were coming so low that they actually cast a shadow across the table, but in order not to alarm Mother we went on with our meal and our chat as if nothing was happening.

The next picture in my mind is conjured up by the sound of endless heavy bombers passing overhead, night after night on the way to London. It was a ghastly, ceaseless drone, and had barely ceased when the returning bombers (which we liked to tell ourselves were fewer in number) came on the scene. Sometimes a single one would circle the house, trying to decide down which chimney to drop its unwanted bombs... On one night we saw a glow in the sky that we knew, or thought we knew, that London was ablaze... Geoffrey was in East London at the time, and it was many days before we heard from him... news came from Janet Good that her flat had been demolished, but she got out a few hours earlier because a time-bomb had fallen in the street in front of the house... an intensely anxious time.

G. H. [Grace] was cooking for the staff at Westminster Hospital. She had a few hours off duty, and in order to make the most of them, she boarded a bus which was already in motion. Result a badly broken leg. She tells of her feeling of impotence when an air raid was going on and she was literally "tied by the leg". When she was cast in plaster, she was sent down to us to recover, with instructions to report at the hospital on a certain day to see whether the plaster could be removed. I arranged to take her up by bus. The night before our expedition, the bombers passed over the house wave after wave, and it seemed as if London must be in ruins, but with the morning it seemed best to carry out our plan unless we were turned back. I shall never forget that drive. As we approached London the familiar route was constantly forsaken, and a diversion made. The wheels of the coach crunched through broken glass... and everywhere houses were heaps of rubble... But the most magnificent sight was that of women standing with children in their arms, on doorsteps which was all that was left of their houses, talking calmly to their neighbours, doing what they could to get a meal together for the family and prepare to spend another ghastly night in the road shelters which seemed to have stood the test nobly. We arrived at Victoria to find the bus station in partial ruins... the restaurant was still functioning, but we had to share the last cup of tea as no more hot water was available... No taxis to be got in spite of my invalid's obvious incapacity (she was on crutches)... arrival at Westminster to find the out-patients department was closed, and while waiting on the off chance of speaking to one of the doctors she knew, I overheard a young doctor say to another in a low voice, "By God, I never knew so much glass could get into so many people". Ambulance after ambulance lined the approach to the hospital. Were they full of dead bodies, or of people waiting their turn for attention? At last I got my patient back to Victoria to await the return bus. There was an enormous queue of people trying to get a ticket out of London, but all seats were booked. I was able to give my ticket to a blind man whose people were trying to send him away, but the face of a girl who could not get a place, and who evidently had been through a very bad time haunts me to this day. After seeing G.H. settle in, with the knowledge that she would be met at Rolvenden, I set off to try to get down to Blackheath to see a friend. It took me about four hours to get there, and my relief was enormous when I found her safe and sound, though she had put out dozens of incendiaries in her garden the previous night.

Now came the fear of invasion. What were we to do with our aged parent? The first step we took was to make her a bedroom on the ground floor, where she was as safe as it was possible to make it, so that we should not disturb her at night. Would the best thing be to put her into her chair and go as far off the roads...

[Dorothy's record was incomplete, and this marks the end of the surviving text.]

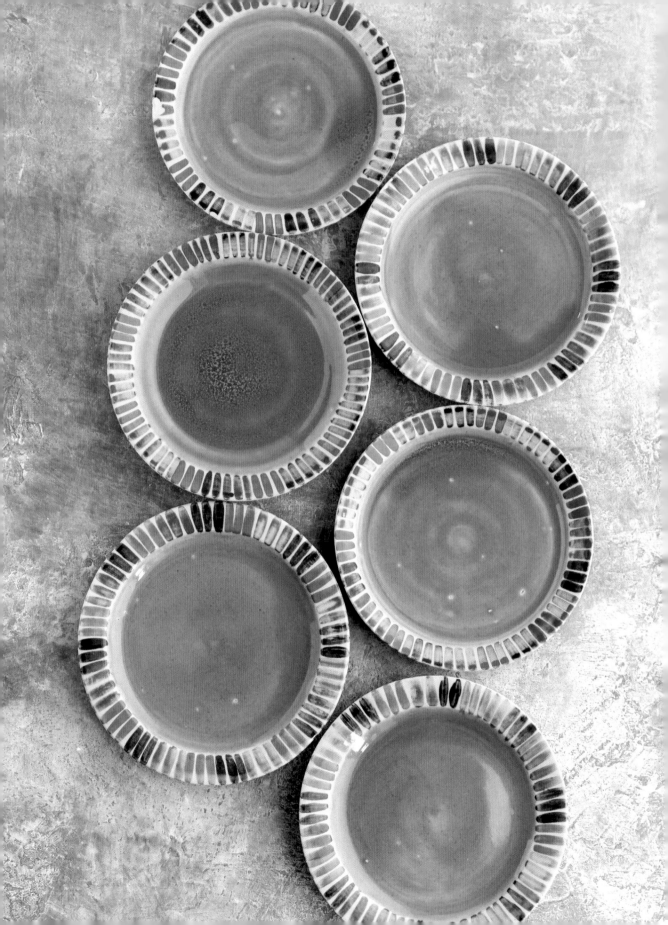

CHAPTER 6

Rolvenden Revival

I t is unclear when restrictions were lifted after the cessation of hostilities in May 1945, and when Dorothy was able to restart The Bridge Pottery. When she did, now aged fifty seven, there were some notable differences from the optimistic pre-war years. From now on, family setbacks and concerns about succession arose on top of her ongoing financial worries. Yet in the forthcoming years she produced some of her most attractive and successful pottery.

Dorothy had written that she was nearly penniless when she arrived in Rolvenden in 1935 yet had to incur all the costs of re-establishing her pottery and new home. With only four years before the conflict, there can't have been much chance to recoup her investment in advance of the enforced closure. Although she gained from her mother's estate in 1942 and from the subsequent sub-letting of Lime House, it is unlikely that she entered the last phase of her pottery with strong finances.

When she was able to resume work, Dorothy developed a pleasingly evolved and simplified range of wares characterised by circular bands of decoration in blues, greens, purples and browns, with subtly complementary inner glazes. She considered these simple, clean and bright designs to be in harmony with the post-war mood. As before, her clay was sent down by Fulham Pottery and her paints and glazes were ordered from the commercial pottery suppliers Messrs Wenger of Stoke-on-Trent.

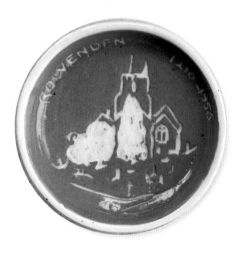

◄ **Decorative plates**

▶ **Commemorative bowl 'Rolvenden 1216 - 1956'**

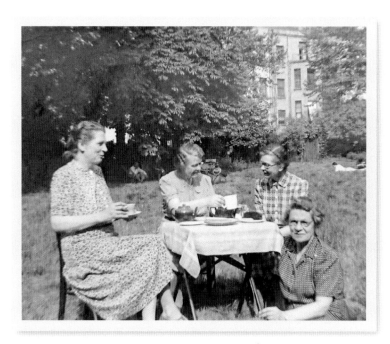

▲ Teatime in high summer 1945. Dorothy and Ethel (centre left and right) with Janet and Margery Good each side. This much treasured last photograph of the sisters together was most likely taken near Albert Road, Regent's Park, London where the Goods lived

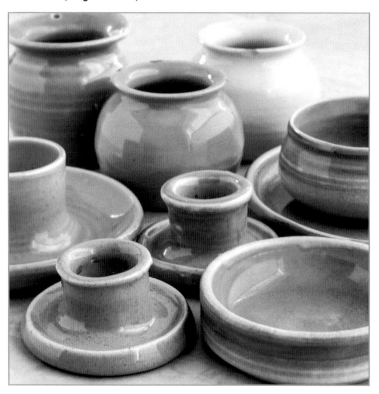

▲ Plain tones for the post-war years

The first post-war loss Dorothy had to cope with was Ethel's sudden death, at the age of fifty nine, on 30 January 1946. Ethel had moved back to the pottery six months before she had a heart attack. Dorothy sent a telegram to Geoffrey and his wife Kathleen who were in Sheffield, and they rushed down by overnight train to be with her when she died in Ashford Hospital the following morning. Later, Dorothy wrote about the 'family disease' which had claimed Ethel and to which her father and brother Arthur's deaths had been attributed. From her correspondence, this worry understandably played on her mind. Ethel's death must have been a great setback as not only did it mean an end to their weaving and pottery partnership, but the end of their years of affectionate companionship. Towards the end of her life, Dorothy wrote that she had always adored Ethel, who from the moment she was born had adored her. A photograph of the sisters with friends having tea in a London park taken just a few months before Ethel died reveals her frailty. Dorothy had a copy of this image enlarged and held it especially dear.

Ethel left £1,127 17s 1d to Dorothy in her will. Her loom was moved to Geoffrey and Kathleen's home in nearby High Halden and the weaving shed was cleared out to make a guest room. With Ethel's loom, yarns and contacts, Geoffrey and Kathleen established Fairwarp Weavers. Their enterprise grew to become one of the largest employers in High Halden, producing garments such as skirts and scarves, as well as table mats and cloths to sell alongside Bridge pottery as

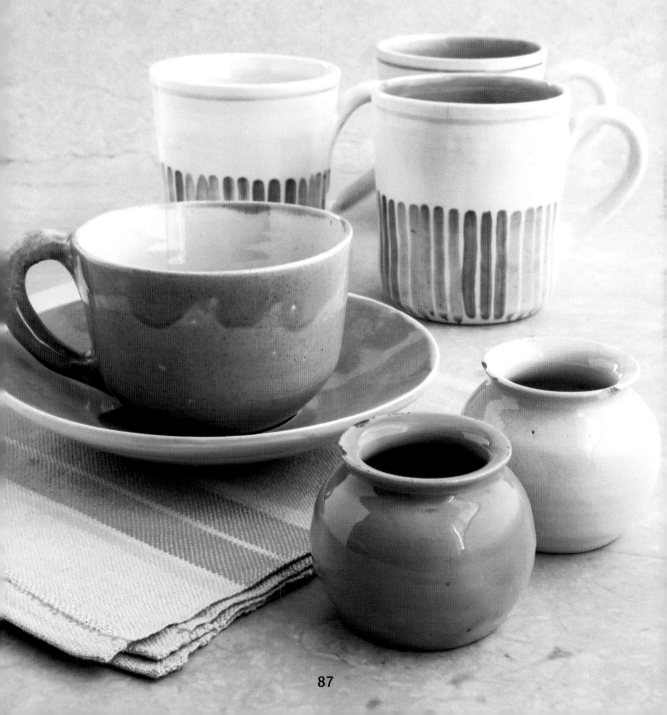

Post-war simplicity of Dorothy's designs, including one of Miss Thoburn's green cups and saucers bought as seconds

Ethel had done before. Fairwarp continued to supply many of the same stores that Dorothy and Ethel had got to know, including Harlequins in Bexhill, and continued to display pottery and textiles together at local fairs.

The following year, on 14 September 1947, Dorothy's oldest brother Frederick died in Philadelphia. He had first moved to the United States after the Great War to take up a consular appointment and had been appointed Consul General to Philadelphia in 1919. Frederick returned most years before the war and had last visited Dorothy at Lime House in 1938.

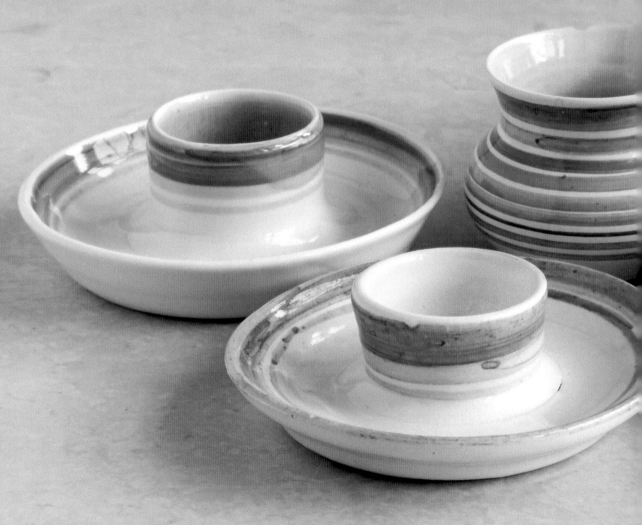

Breakfast set

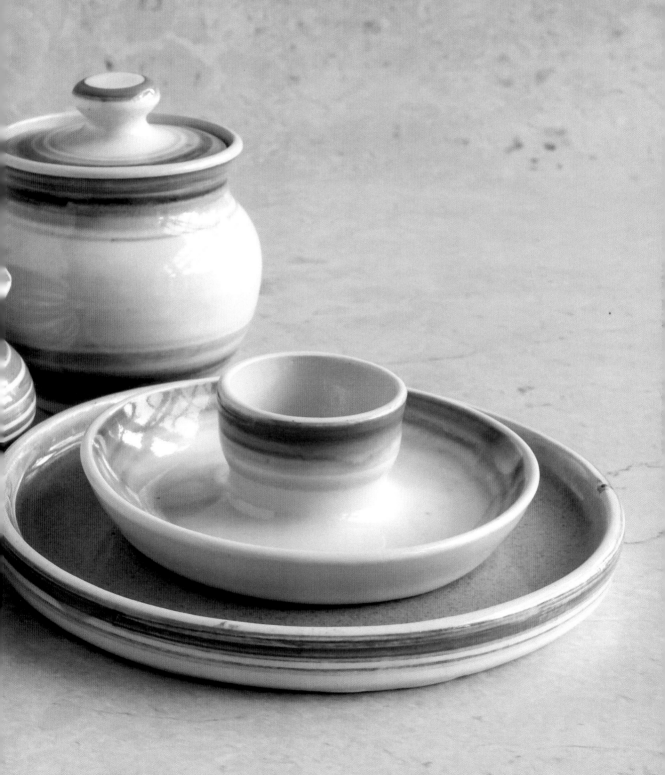

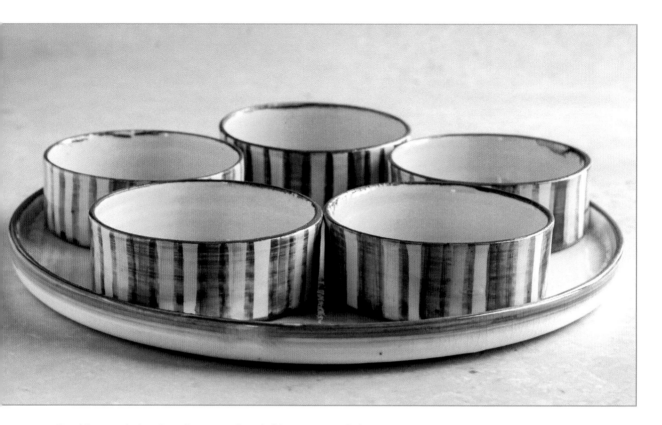

▲ For this commission, Dorothy reverted to a bolder pattern and glaze, reminiscent of her Beauworth designs

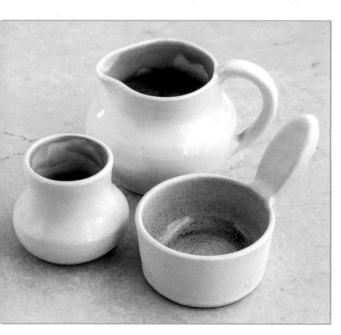

▲ Unfinished experimental pieces and, to the right, with an unsuccessful inner glaze

Once Dorothy had re-established The Bridge Pottery, it again became a point of interest in the village. Dorothy especially sought to encourage young people to come in and try her craft. Betty Weller recalls from her childhood, that when she delivered milk to the pottery, she would have a little play with the clay before moving on. George Babbage remembers being invited to try out pottery as part of a group from Rolvenden Village School. He did not have the impression that the pottery was particularly active just after the war and there were only a few items on display in the showroom. When he returned on his own, he had to knock on the door to get in as the pottery was normally closed: 'In the evenings, the village policeman used to wait with his bicycle in the sheltered pottery entrance for his sergeant to come along.'

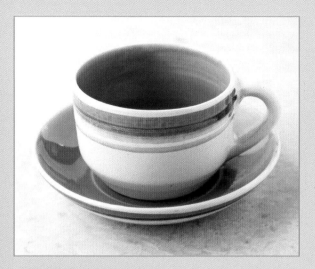

▲ Breakfast cup and saucer

▲ Egg cups

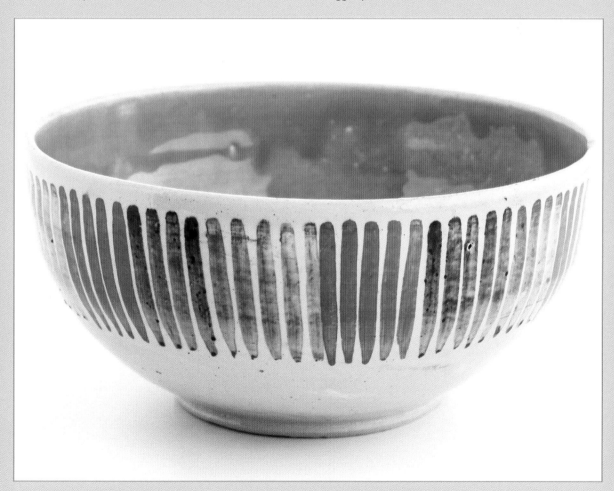

▲ Fruit bowl

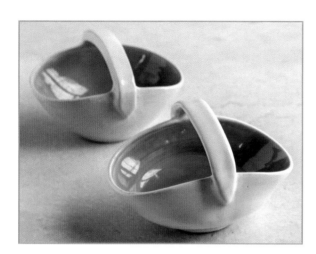

▲ **Fruit baskets**

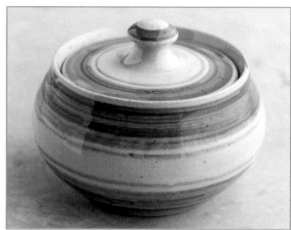

▲ **Sugar bowl with lid**

Betty Pool-Mathers also recalled visiting from school:

We used to go down there in our lunch hour from school and she showed us how to make things. We'd have a try at a pot or cup and the handle would come off. She liked us to have a go; she liked to show us things. It was like a lesson; she wouldn't let us play with all that clay or muck about. We used to get this old muck on our hands and throw it onto the thing and put your hand in the middle and shape it from scratch. There were Miss Watson and another lady.

In the late 1940s the village had about fifteen shops and small businesses. The pottery was different from most as it sold items that were more desirable than strictly necessary. People travelled to Rolvenden to see what they might buy.

Elizabeth and Patricia Barham, girls who lived opposite the pottery at Saxbys, recall having pottery lessons and their mother Peggy (Mrs Harold) Barham was a supporter and friend.

Maggie Sim, who spent part of her childhood at Lime House after her aunt, Audrey Davis, had taken on the lease, recalls that the house was 'very basic and cold'. She often visited the pottery and was always welcome as Dorothy was 'very sweet, easy' and fond of children. 'In the pottery, there was a big room where Dorothy lived with an old-fashioned roll-top desk. Everything lived in there, including a pack of cards which she used to get out.'

Similarly, whilst living at Lime Cottage as children in the early 1950s, Annabel and Mary Steele used to visit 'Watsie', as she was affectionately known. They learnt to play cards. Charlotte Molesworth also visited as a child: 'The shelves were packed with pots in tight rows stacked high at different stages of drying; biscuit fired before being glazed and becoming the finished articles.' Charlotte was allowed to make pots in the school holidays and described Dorothy as small and neat. 'She always wore marvellous button-up brown overalls. She was kind and obviously patient but was always busy working there on her own.'

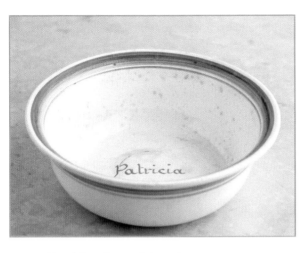

▲ Cereal bowl for Miss Patricia Barham

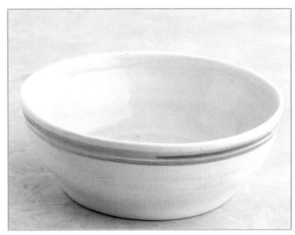

▲ Fruit bowl

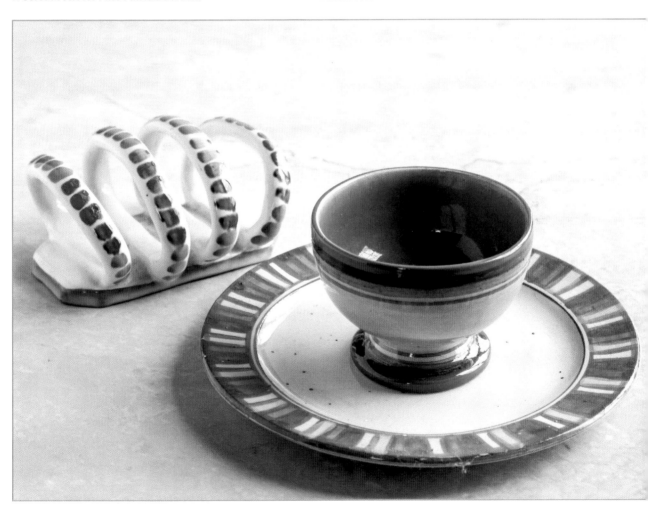

▲ The simplicity of Dorothy's 1950s toast rack contrasts with her heavier work from Beauworth in the 1920s and '30s

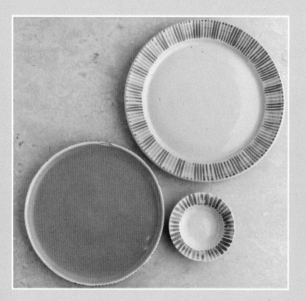

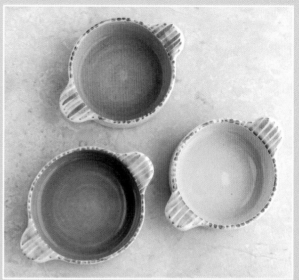

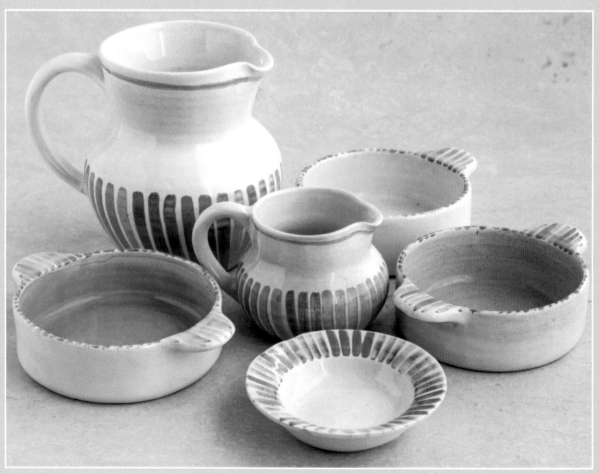

▲ ▶ Bridge Pottery perfection, 1950s

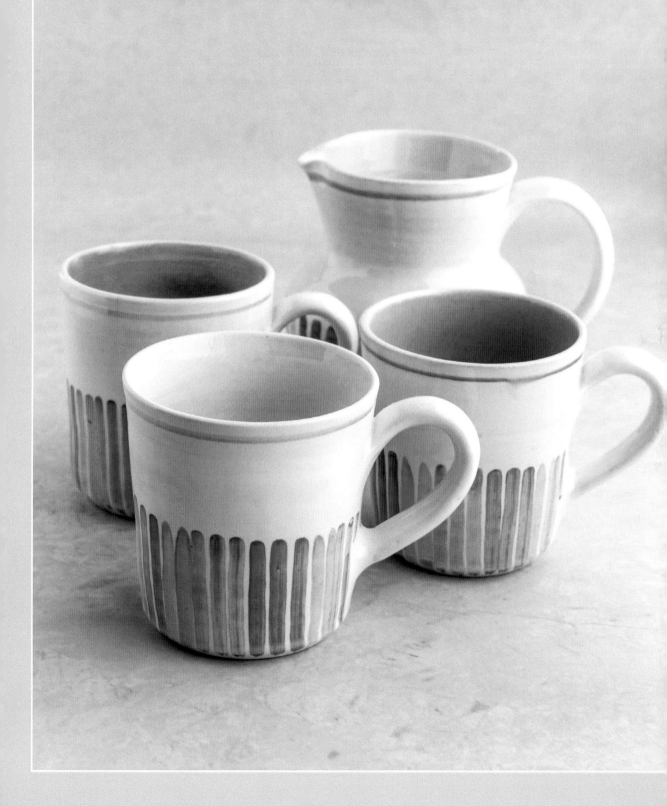

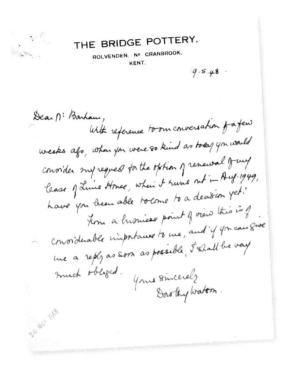

▲ **Letter to Hole Park Estate, 19 May 1948**

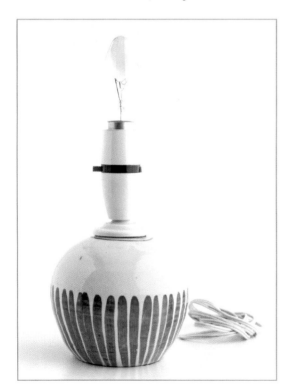

▲ **Table lamp**

Despite many reasons for pride in the success and appreciation of her wares, worries about her finances and succession were never far away. In May 1948 Dorothy revealed her anxiety to Colonel Barham of Hole Park when she wrote about renewing her lease which was due to expire the following year. She felt it imperative that she should retain the lease on Lime House, not only for the income but to have it available for any business partner or successor who she hoped would come along. Dorothy wrote:

> *Apart from the workshops and my small dwelling, which is of vital importance to my business, Lime House seems to be the only possible abode for an assistant or partner, of whom I shall have increasing need as the years go on. I am very glad to let it to Mrs Davies as she is working for me, but should she leave it, it is important to me to let some other assistant have it. The only way I can keep it for this purpose is to sub-let it partially furnished, as I am doing at the moment, for a very low rent.*

The need for this important provision was recognised and a new lease for fourteen years was agreed in 1949 at a rent of £75 for the first seven years, and £85 thereafter.

Unfortunately, difficulties arose again and about eighteen months later had reached the point at which Dorothy decided to give up and sell the pottery as a going concern. This may have coincided with concerns for her health as by then Grace and Henry were also unwell and she saw her future with her brother John who was ten years younger. She wrote to Colonel Barham on 8 February 1951 to tell him:

> *Various reasons make it desirable that I should leave Rolvenden and go and live with my brother [John] and consequently I propose to endeavour to sell the goodwill and equipment of my pottery and am having the value of the same assessed.*

After his service with The Royal Engineers during the Second World War, John had returned to India where he had previously worked as a railway bridge engineer to help prepare India Railways for independence. He returned and took up market gardening at Horsham in East Sussex. Of all her brothers, John was the closest and Dorothy's letter reveals that she planned to move and live with him. With a plan in mind, a pamphlet was produced to sell the business as a going concern. The particulars reveal another pressure that perhaps contributed to Dorothy's decision: 'that the small pottery had become so well-known and so popular that it was quite impossible to meet the demand for its productions'.

The response to this sales initiative is unknown. However, Dorothy was able to write a much brighter letter to Hole Park Estate on 8 July 1951 to explain a change of mind. 'Now that my plans are getting more settled… it seems unlikely that I shall have to uproot

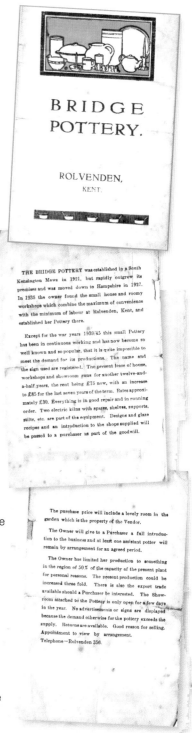

▲ The Bridge Pottery sales particulars, 1951

THE BRIDGE POTTERY was established in a South Kensington Mews in 1921, but rapidly outgrew its premises and was moved down to Hampshire in 1927. In 1935 the owner found the small house and roomy workshops which combine the maximum of convenience with the minimum of labour at Rolvenden, Kent, and established the pottery there.

Except for the war years 1939/45 this small Pottery has been in continuous working and has now become so well-known and so popular, that it is quite impossible to meet the demand for its products. The name and the sign are registered. The present lease of house, workshops and showroom runs for another twelve-and-a-half-years, the rent being £75 now, with an increase to £85 for the last seven years of the term. Rates approximately £20. Everything is in good repair and in running order. Two electric kilns with spares, shelves, supports, stilts, etc. are part of the equipment. Designs of the glaze recipes and an introduction to the shops supplied will be passed to a purchaser as part of the goodwill.

The purchase price will include a lovely room in the garden which is the property of the Vendor.

The owner will give to a purchaser a full introduction to the business and at least one assistant potter will remain by arrangement for an agreed period.

The owner has limited her production to something in the region of 50% of the capacity of the present plant for personal reasons. The present production could be increased three fold. There is also the export trade available should a Purchaser be interested. The Showroom attached to the property is only open for a few days in the year. No advertisements or signs are displayed because the demand otherwise for the pottery exceeds the supply. Returns are available. Good reason for selling. Appointments to view by arrangement.

Telephone – Rolvenden 356.

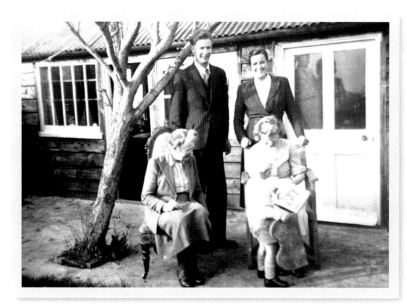

▲ Family group in 1950. Back row: nephew Geoffrey Watson (left) and niece Ursula Watson (right). Front row: Dortohy Watson (left) and Kathleen Watson (right) with great nephew Paul. Behind is the west end of the pottery building, the door on the left leading into Dorothy's kitchen and the one on the right into her sitting room

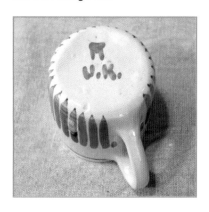

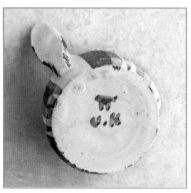

▲ Bridge mark with the addition of 'UK'

myself from Rolvenden.' This may have corresponded with John's decision to stop market gardening, which was not successful, and return to his engineering expertise. He took up a position with London Underground working for their Bridge Engineering Department, and in due course moved to live near Kew. However, there were still thoughts that he would spend weekends with Dorothy as she wrote to Colonel Barham to ask if a garage could be put up for his car.

Having got through this hurdle, The Bridge Pottery continued under Dorothy in Rolvenden for another decade, although it was quieter in its latter years when she worked much of the time alone. Her nephew Stephen recalls that she had a frugal existence as, for example, there was no fireplace in her pottery rooms, few home comforts or bookshelves or books. Although frustrated not to be able to do all the things she had done before, she remained determined and very much her own mistress who liked to be in control. Samples were created marked 'UK' and 'Rolvenden' beneath her pottery mark, which suggests that she may have had an eye on sales in France as well as developing a higher profile in Kent. There is no information to confirm that she ever shipped to France, but she had referred to the export potential in her sales pamphlet, and with her fluent French had stayed in touch with families from her early travels there.

At some point Dorothy hoped to persuade David Watson, one of Arthur's sons, to join her. She offered him a position, insisting that he serve a seven-year apprenticeship. This would seem excessive, especially as she had trained under Dora Lunn for only two years, but she was so eager to secure her succession that she may have wanted to tie him in. However, as David's nephew Richard Torrance reflected: 'Having been a major in the Second War, and certainly fighting through Italy, he would not have relished taking orders from his aunt for seven years and decided to seek his fortune elsewhere. He went into interior design.'

Unfortunately, Dorothy also had to cope with further family setbacks. Firstly, Ursula, who had spent some of her childhood staying with her in Beauworth and Rolvenden, contracted polio whilst expecting her second child. She died on 7 September 1952.

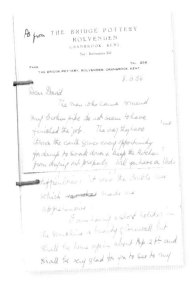
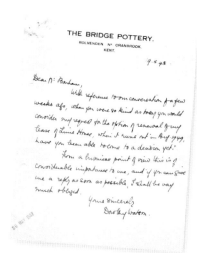
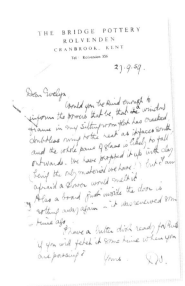

▲ **Examples of Bridge Pottery letterheads**

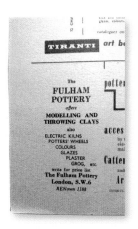
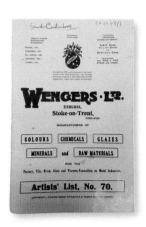
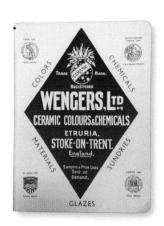
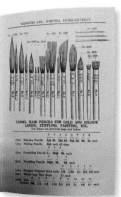
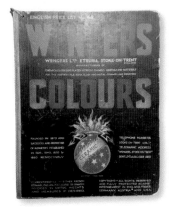
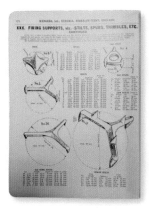

▲ **Suppliers of materials to The Bridge Pottery**

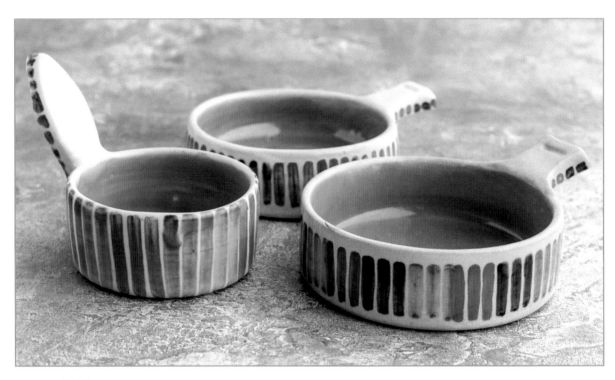

▲ Assorted dishes

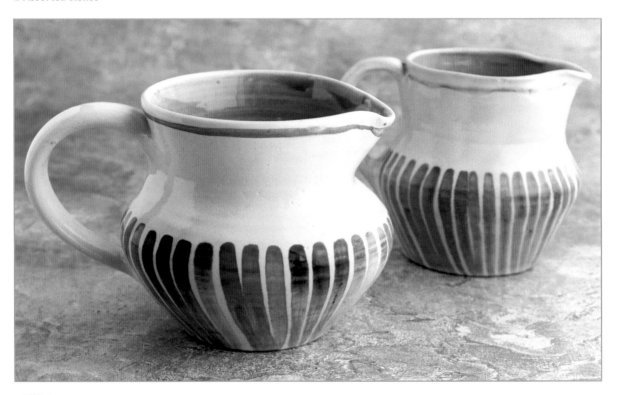

▲ Milk jugs

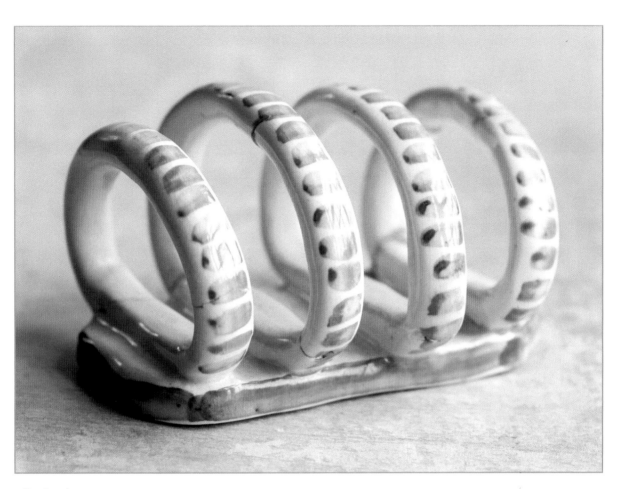

▲ Toast rack

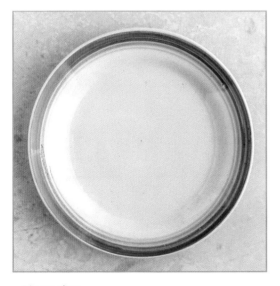

▲ Dinner plate

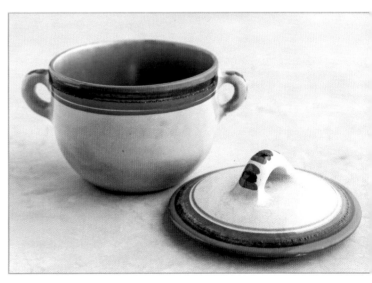

▲ Jam pot with lid

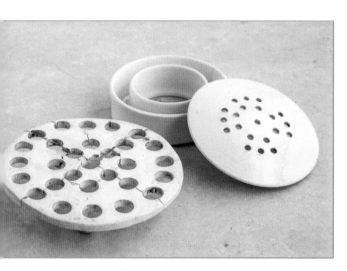

▲ Trivet with wild-flower vase

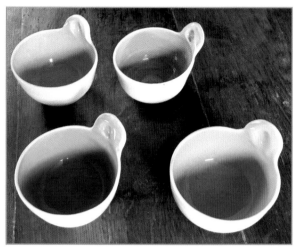

▲ Soup or porridge bowls

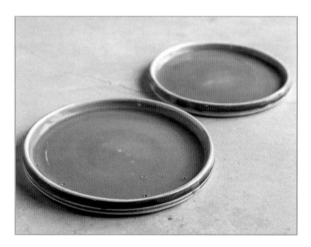

▲ Serving trays

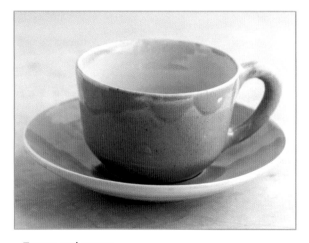

▲ Tea cup and saucer

Then there was great sadness when Grace died on 28 February 1954, aged sixty three, from the 'family disease'. She had returned to live at the pottery after giving up her wartime cooking job in London but died whilst staying at Hove in East Sussex. She left Dorothy £1,483 in her will.

Before these deaths, Dorothy had forged a link with the Christian community of St Julian at Coolham, in West Sussex. The community had been founded by the redoubtable Florence Allshorn in 1941 to offer respite to Christians, missionaries and low-income families.

It opened a children's home at Farley's House, near Hailsham, in East Sussex. It is unclear what attracted Dorothy, but she had a great deal to cope with on her own and may have found comfort through the companionship of like-minded women. Florence Allshorn was always in great need of money to fund the community, but it is unlikely that Dorothy had much to spare. At times, both Geoffrey and Ursula had stayed at Farley's House and in due course Ursula had become more involved and met her husband through the community.

Undaunted, Dorothy experimented with glazes as well as new shapes and pieces. Her great nephew, Paul Watson, recalls that 'Dod made a set of nativity figures for us and

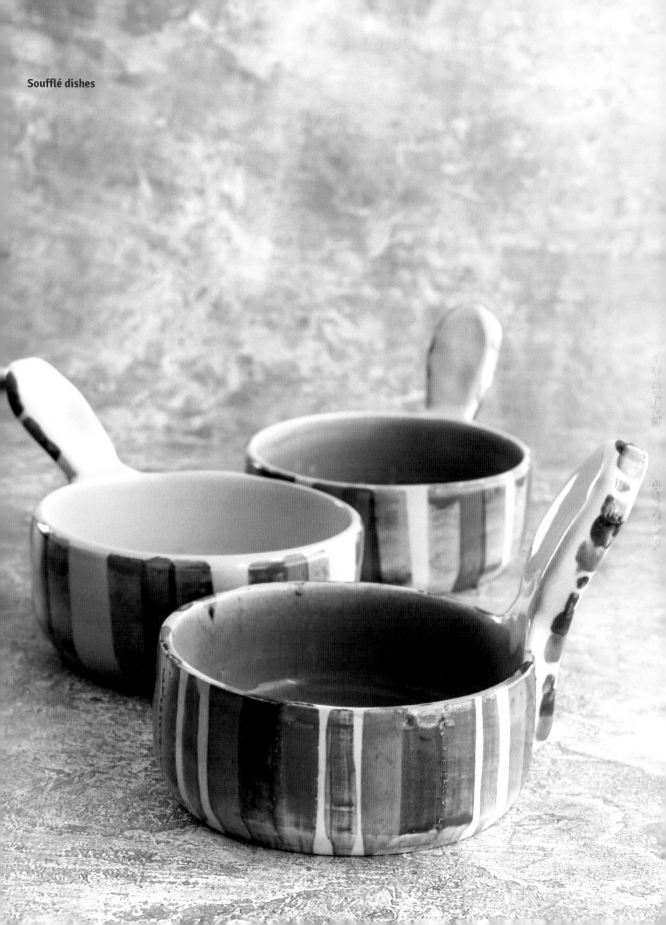

Soufflé dishes

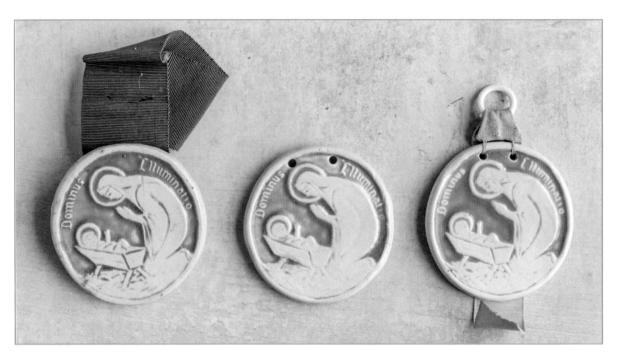

▲ 'Dominus Illuminati' Christmas decorations with ribbon attachments, late 1950s, with Sister Margaret CR of the Community of the Resurrection of Our Lord in mind

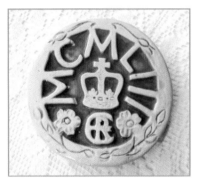

▲ Coronation medallion, Elizabeth II, 2 June 1953

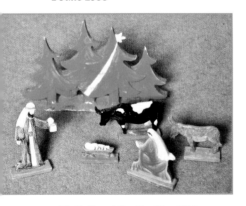

▲ Nativity set for Geoffrey Watson and his family, late 1950s

each year my mother would take the books out of one shelf of the bookcase and set the figures on new shapes and pieces'. She produced medallions for the Coronation of Queen Elizabeth II in 1953 and Christmas tree decorations with the lettering 'Dominus Illuminati' in pale blue above a crib.

In the 1950s and perhaps under less pressure, Dorothy was able to travel again. She joined Audrey Davis on a holiday to the Alps. She was left with her easel while the rest of the party set off hiking, and they collected her on the way back. She was photographed in August 1956 with another group of friends in Bavaria, including Madeline Lawrence who was later to join her at the pottery. With her good French, Dorothy also supplemented her income by doing translation work. Between about 1955 and 1958 she also helped as a French teacher at Benenden School for Girls in the next village. Her neighbour, Miss Penelope Cox, was Art Mistress and Madeline Lawrence also helped at the school part-time, teaching pottery and Art. Another new aspect for Dorothy during this phase of the pottery, now that she had a guest room, was to take in students to learn pottery skills.

As she had done before, Dorothy undertook commissions including commemorative items for christenings or retirements. These included an inscribed jug as a leaving gift for Rolvenden's schoolmistress in 1956. Child-sized christening mugs were made to order.

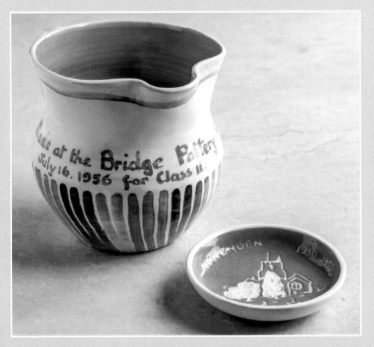

▲ Commemorative pieces for 'Class II of Rolvenden School, 16 July 1956' and for 'Rolvenden 1216 - 1956'

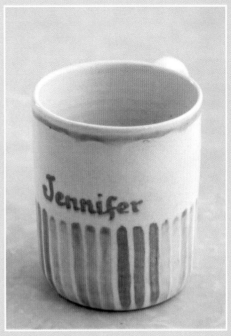

▲ Christening mug for Miss Jennifer Barham, 1957

By 1958, Dorothy was seventy, but still very active. Paul Watson recalls the pottery at this time:

The shed was a long, fairly narrow building on the road with a big front entrance and sign outside. The shop front door was recessed and on each side of it were display windows for her wares. Going in the front door, the pottery was on the left and the first thing one saw was the electric kiln on legs on the left and trays of 'biscuit' waiting to be glazed and fired. Further down, the potter's wheels. From the front door, if you turned right you would be in Dod's sitting room and beyond that was her kitchen and presumably her bedroom. I suppose that in earlier days, when they all lived in Lime House, this was all also a potting area.

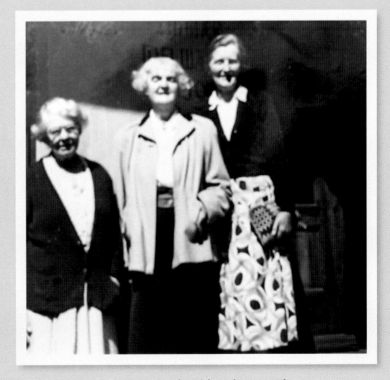

▲ Holiday party in Bavaria. Dorothy with Madge Lee and Madeline Lawrence, August 1956

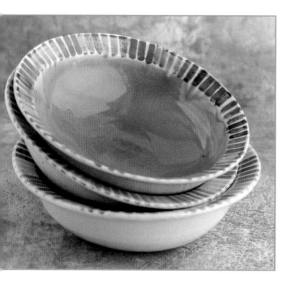

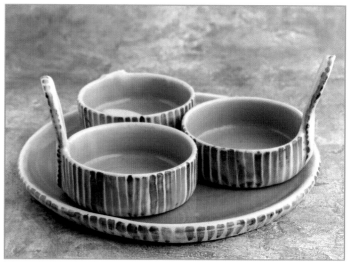

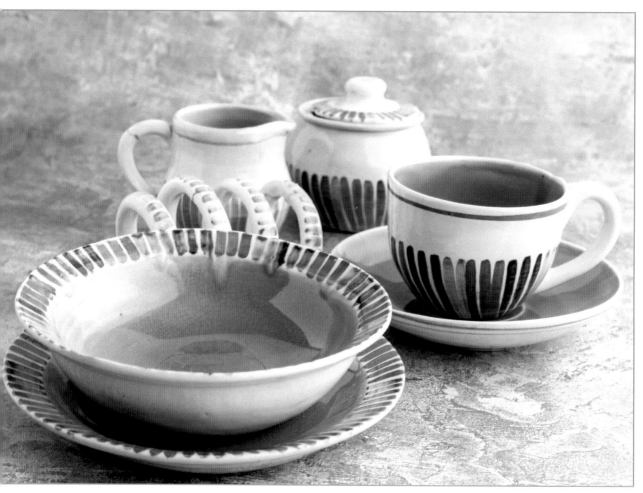

▲ ▶ Concluding pieces from The Bridge Pottery, Rolvenden in the late 1950s

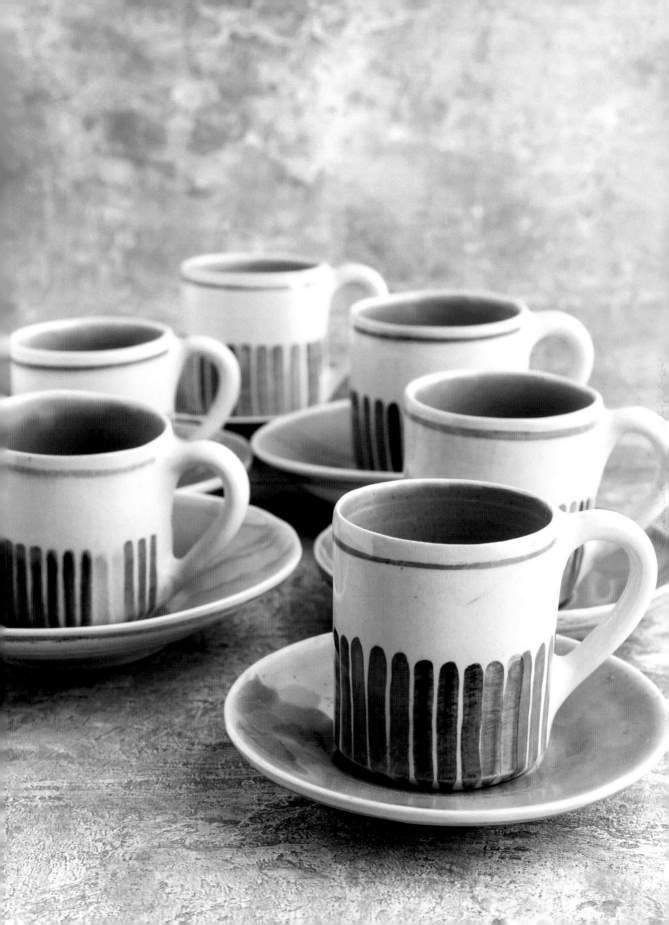

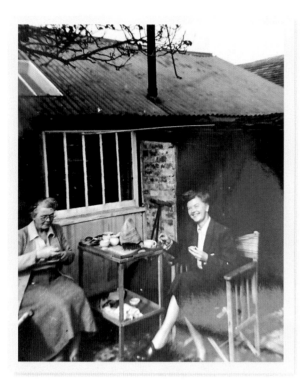

▲ Dorothy having tea with a student potter in the 1950s.
Note the poor condition of the pottery behind

Increasingly though, in her final pottery years, Dorothy found it a struggle to keep up with demand and opened the showroom less often. She still, however, held an annual show of seconds and surplus stock as she had done all along. Rolvenden villagers recall that by the late 1950s there was little activity in the pottery, yet the momentum picked up when Dorothy was joined by Madeline 'Maddie' Lawrence some time before 1957. Madeline had been living with her sister until they sold their parents' farm, whereupon she moved to live in a caravan in Biddenden until she could find another property. Dorothy may have hoped that with her capital, she was well placed to take over the pottery as a going concern. It must have been some relief for Dorothy when Madeline moved into Lime House during 1957 and began to help her in the pottery. Two years later the *Kent Messenger* newspaper visited and published a feature on them both at work.

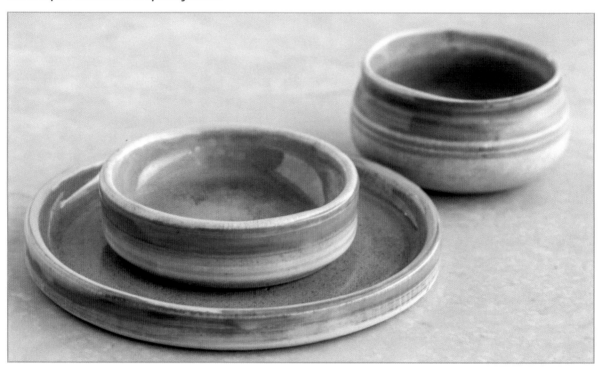

▲ Assorted pieces

KENT MESSENGER, November 20, 1959
They practice the old rural crafts

Basically the same as rural crafts practiced in medieval times, examples of table ware made by the Bridge Pottery at Rolvenden, and of garments from High Halden, will be on show at the Old Palace, Maidstone on Monday and Tuesday in support of the exhibition of monumental brass rubbings on view in the main hall.

"I took up pottery making after the first war, and have been at it ever since," said Miss Dorothy Watson, principal of the Bridge Pottery.

"The demand is still as great as ever, for hand-made pottery never loses its individuality."

Helping Miss Watson part time are Miss E. M. Lawrence (who also teaches at Benenden School) and Mrs J Duval.

Two of the three kilns at the pottery are normally in use, and the articles take roughly 12 hours to "fire". After allowing anther 12 hours in which to cool, they are then coloured and dipped in glaze, after which they are fired for the second time.

The results, apart from their utilitarian use as vases, cups, jugs, ash trays and many other items, are works of art created by the co-ordination of hand and brain at the potter's wheel.

Weaving

With his guardian's ancient loom, Mr G. M. Watson started the firm of Fairwarp Weavers 12 years ago. With his wife doing the sewing, and he himself the weaving, they produce skirts, and scarves that are accepted by shops throughout the country, and their high standard of work is being appreciated in America. Mr Watson now employs four full-time girls who work to original designs produced by him. Multi-coloured scarves are now being produced for the Christmas market, each one takes an hour to make.
In addition to articles of clothing, table mats and cushion covers are also woven.

Another feature of Fairwarp Weavers is the warping drum which was designed by Mr Watson, and made by two local carpenters. The yarn comes from Yorkshire. It is vat dried into special shades.

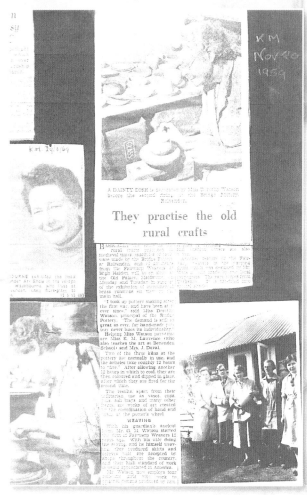

▲ Article, *Kent Messenger*, Phyllis Hook's Scrapbook, 20 November 1959

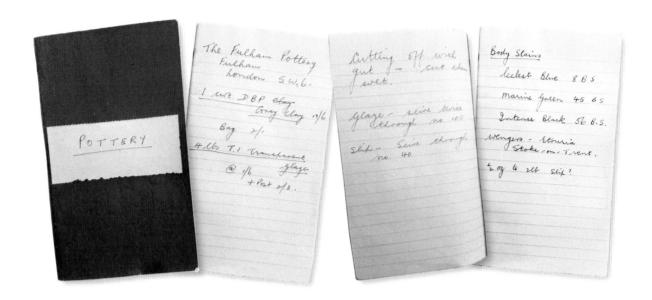

▲ **Dorothy's pottery succession notes for Miss Lawrence**

▾ **Bridge Pottery 40th Annual Christmas Sale card, 1961**

Now that she had a successor, Dorothy could begin to plan her withdrawal whilst continuing to own the business and the lease. She prepared notes about the purchase of supplies and the glazes and paints she used. Betty Weller, one of her assistants, suggests that it was an increase in insurance premium that finally made Dorothy decide that she should leave before the end of 1961. By then, The Bridge Pottery had existed in Rolvenden for twenty six years and it was forty years since Dorothy had first started on her own as a potter in Sumner Place Mews. By this time Dorothy was aged seventy three. With the satisfaction of knowing that Madeline would succeed her, Dorothy prepared for her final and 40th Annual Christmas Sale.

Dorothy left Rolvenden almost immediately after the sale, spending a few days over Christmas with Geoffrey and Kathleen in High Halden before moving on. She had made clear to Hole Park Estate that she wanted to retain control of the pottery and Lime House leases, even though Madeline Lawrence was in situ, until the conclusion of her agreement in August 1963.

The Bridge Pottery

1921 - 1961

40th Annual Christmas Sale

with

The Fairwarp Weavers

on

Saturday 25th November 1961

10 a.m. - 4 p.m.

and following week while stocks last

110

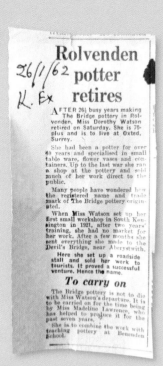

Rolvenden potter retires

26/1/62 K. Ex

AFTER 26½ busy years making The Bridge pottery in Rolvenden, Miss Dorothy Watson retired on Saturday. She is 70-plus and is to live at Oxted, Surrey.

She had been a potter for over 40 years and specialised in small table ware, flower vases and containers. Up to the last war she ran a shop at the pottery and sold much of her work direct to the public.

Many people have wondered how the registered name and trade mark of The Bridge pottery originated.

When Miss Watson set up her first small workshop in South Kensington in 1921, after two years' training, she had no market for her work. After a few months she sent everything she made to the Devil's Bridge, near Aberystwith.

Here she set up a roadside stall and sold her work to tourists. It proved a successful venture. Hence the name.

To carry on

The Bridge pottery is not to die with Miss Watson's departure. It is to be carried on for the time being by Miss Madeline Lawrence, who has helped to produce it for the past seven years.

She is to combine the work with teaching pottery at Benenden School.

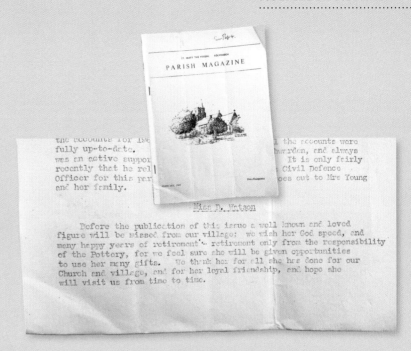

PARISH MAGAZINE

...the accounts for 19.. fully up-to-date. ...was an active suppor... recently that he rel... Officer for this par... and her family.

...l the accounts were ...hwarden, and always It is only fairly ...Civil Defence ...oes out to Mrs Young

Miss D. Watson

Before the publication of this issue a well known and loved figure will be missed from our village; we wish her God speed, and many happy years of retirement - retirement only from the responsibility of the Pottery, for we feel sure she will be given opportunities to use her many gifts. We thank her for all she has done for our Church and village, and for her loyal friendship, and hope she will visit us from time to time.

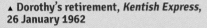

▲ Dorothy's retirement, *Kentish Express*, 26 January 1962

▲ Dorothy's retirement announcement in *Rolvenden Parish Magazine*, 1962

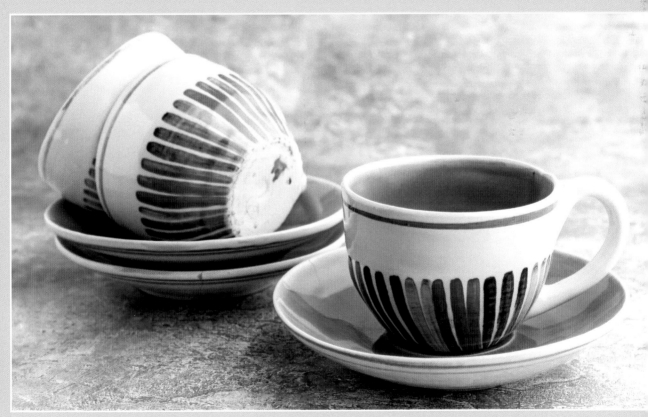

▲ Tea cups and saucers

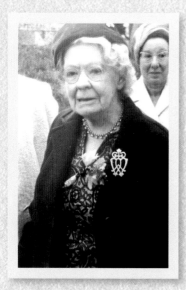
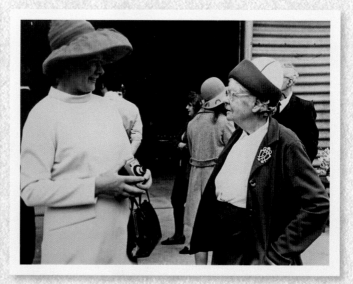
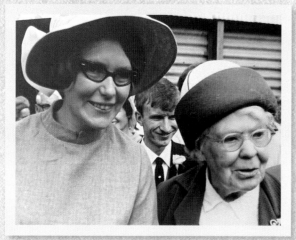
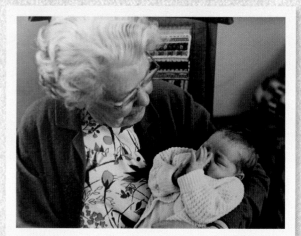
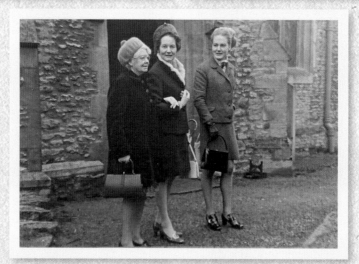

CHAPTER 7

Later Years

I n a brave decision, by early 1962 Dorothy had moved away from her family and the community she had known for the past twenty eight years, to go to Blunt House in Oxted. This was about forty miles away, just over the border into Surrey. Notwithstanding any relief she may have felt, this must have been an unsettling time as she adjusted to retirement, living as part of the community in the large neo-Georgian house. She also had to wrestle with the dilemma of extracting herself from all the buzz and day-to-day pressures of The Bridge Pottery, and yet, no doubt, continuing to feel responsible for its future.

Her great nephew Stephen recalls from his visits, that although in good health, Dorothy was frustrated by the change and spoke through gritted teeth. She complained that she had little to do. She must have thought it best to move some distance away from Rolvenden, but in doing so, she left her friends and activities behind, such as her regular game of bridge. She tried to busy herself with domestic chores helping the staff but was seemingly ill at ease. She must have been delighted when Madeline asked her to return for a few weeks in July 1962 to help in the pottery.

For some years, Dorothy had supplemented her income by doing French translation work. And she had kept up contact with the family in Bavay. Perhaps influenced by the BBC's project of making available recordings of English nursery rhymes on vinyl discs to play to young children on the Continent, Dorothy decided on a new idea. She would do likewise. Under the banner 'The Bridge Voices', she made a speculative recording of nursery rhymes on reel-to-reel tapes that was then transposed onto vinyl discs, which she hoped to sell.

◄ A selection of family pictures from Dorothy's later years. Clockwise from top left: Dorothy Watson with her Lockhart Brooch; Mary Watson talking to her aunt Dorothy on 3 May 1969; Dorothy with her great-great niece Annabel Watson (aged two weeks) taken on 4 May 1969 by Meg Loughborough (Dorothy's niece); Dorothy on the arm of her niece by marriage Britta Watson, and her great niece Tina Watson; Dorothy with her great niece Gillian Green at Sacrewell Farm, Wansford, on her wedding day 3 May 1969

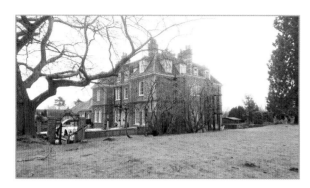

▴ **Blunt House, Oxted, in 2018**

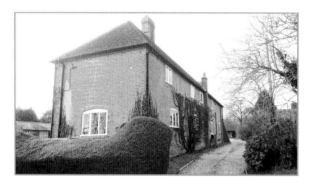

▴ **Brecklands, Lower Froyle, in 2018**

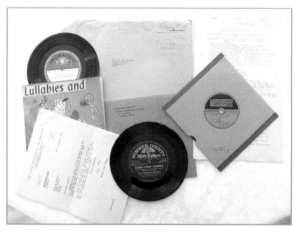

▴ **The Bridge Voices project artefacts, 1961-63**

In January 1963, her recording was most unfavourably critiqued by one possible purchaser, The Folk University of Sweden, and the project did not progress. Using the same word that she had used to describe her brief move to Somerset in 1934, she scrawled 'fiasco' to describe her time at Blunt House.

By June 1963, John had made out a covenant to support her, and Dorothy clearly sought to regain her independence. She soon left Oxted and moved much further west to Lower Froyle in Hampshire, a small village about five miles south-west of Farnham. She moved to No 2, Brecklands, in the village centre, which had previously been a workhouse.

Madeline Lawrence continued to live at Lime House and run the pottery throughout 1962 and seemingly made plans with Dorothy for the enterprise to continue beyond her proprietorship. However, for unknown reasons this was not to be and no new lease with Hole Park Estate was agreed. In any event, given that Madeline was a similar age to Dorothy, it is unlikely that she would have been able to contribute the energy that Dorothy showed when she set up in Rolvenden in 1935 with such an exciting flourish. By this time the equipment and buildings, as well as pottery production and sales, were likely have needed thoroughly reinvigorating. Madeline closed the pottery and moved on 22 October 1962 to Lamberhurst.

Dorothy then sub-let Lime House for a final time until April 1963 which was to be the end of her involvement. She arranged for Ethel's weaving shed to be dismantled and returned her tenancy. She wrote to David Barham saying, 'How very sorry I am to be discontinuing my connection with Rolvenden after 28 strenuous but happy years'.

The pottery buildings stood empty alongside the road and her great nephew Stephen Watson recalls passing them daily on his way to Cranbrook School, gazing at the sad sight from his bus. The electric kiln, along with some of Dorothy's furniture and effects, were still in there in October 1963, as were bits of 'china' which Dorothy had left, hoping that they might be sold for the benefit of the village youth club. One of her potter's wheels was installed in Geoffrey and Kathleen's cottage at Poorsfield, High Halden, together with a tin of clay.

In early 1963 Kent County Council granted permission for the pottery sheds to be demolished to make way for a 3/4-bedroom house and garage.

At Brecklands in early July 1964, Dorothy received news from the Reverend Mother at St Peter's Home, Grahamstown that Margaret had died on 29 June, aged eighty five. The sisters had always corresponded, and Margaret had been anxious about Dorothy the day before she died. This left John and Dorothy as the only remaining siblings. John arranged a Requiem Mass for Margaret at Kew's historic Barn Church. It was held on 11 July and Dorothy attended.

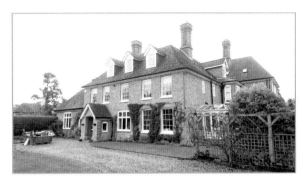

▲ **Dashmonden, Biddenden in 2018**

Some time later Dorothy returned from Lower Froyle to Biddenden to be near Geoffrey and Kathleen again. She took a bed/sitting room in Dashmonden Court, a large 18th-century house on the High Halden Road about half a mile south of the village. Like Blunt House, Dashmonden Court had been divided into residential units and was occupied by people who had returned from the colonies. Dorothy started to do china and pottery

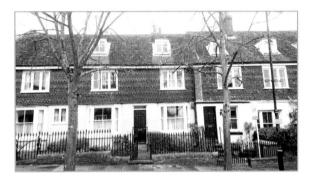

▲ **Fenton House (1st floor, above black painted front door on right), Cranbrook, in 2017**

mending, but none too neatly, judging from the heavy applications of glue on surviving items. Her nephews recall her great enthusiasm for Araldite adhesive and staples to fix broken china, applied with a shaking hand and declining eyesight. Her mind though, was always lively.

Paul Watson recalls that she relied quite heavily on his mother Kathleen to help her get about, which was not always easy as Dorothy was demanding at times. She had found fresh things to focus her energies on, such as campaigning for a pavement from the village. On 27 August 1968, John died at the age of seventy. Dorothy wrote to her nephew Stephen Watson, then living in British Columbia, to explain she felt that 'being ten years younger than me he would surely outlive me, but he died like most of the family from angina and has left me the only surviving member of my generation'.

In the late 1960s, Dorothy moved into Fenton House in the High Street of Cranbrook, where she took a small flat, No 4, at the front on the first floor. Since the early 1960s this property had provided sheltered housing for elderly people. It must have been convenient, with shops just yards away, and from there she carried on mending china. Aware, through her own frailty, that she also had the 'family disease', she had to go slowly, but her great nephews recall that her mind was sharp until the end. Dorothy died on 16 April 1971 aged eighty three.

Her funeral was held on 27 April at St Dunstan's Church in Cranbrook, before the gloomy procession to Charing near Ashford, where her ashes were scattered between oak trees on the west lawn. Of the ten children in her family whose lives stretched for ninety two years from 1879 to 1971, Dorothy had outlived them all.

Forty Years a Potter.

In Canada.

At the Ministry of Shipping.

Dora Lunn — the Ravenscourt Pottery -

In the New.

In Hampshire.

Sold cottages a went to ~~So~~ Somerset - fiasco.

Search for new premises -

Robrendenden.

Retirement to Oxted - fiasco.

Lower Frogle - china . mending.

Priddendus   "   "

Cranbrook.   "   "

CHAPTER 8

Reflections

One may conclude from almost every stage of Dorothy Watson's life, that it was her determination, coupled with her own hands and initiative, from which came the attractive work that enabled The Bridge Pottery to achieve so much.

One wonders what difference it would have made had she enjoyed secure financial backing. Perhaps, as seen with her contemporaries Dora Lunn and Majel Davidson, she may have taken greater risks or allowed her artistic interests to evolve, rather than being bound by the overriding discipline of making what would sell. But that was not to be. Instead, Dorothy spent her life continuously working, always on the go, and constantly seeking opportunities to ease the struggle of producing her lovely wares. Even in retirement she could not rest.

Dorothy Watson's legacy as a studio potter is a body of work appreciated for its simplicity and attractiveness as it evolved through five decades. Her success was to have honed the necessary skills and to have applied them day-in and day-out to create her wares despite her rudimentary set-ups. She remained on trusted ground, adapting to maintain relevance in order to survive. 'Necessity breeds the best work' and perhaps one of her greatest tributes came in her lifetime when she recognised that so sought

◀ **Dorothy, in her own handwriting, succinctly summarises her whole career**

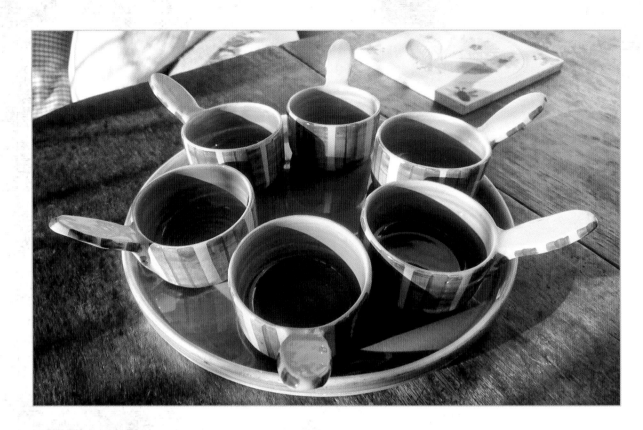

▲▼▶ **Some of Miss Thoburn's Bridge Pottery wares which 'raise your spirits when you see and use them'**

after were her wares, she was simply unable to keep up with demand.

Over time, Dorothy may have simplified what she created but she never took shortcuts or compromised her fundamental value of simply decorated good design.

Behind her at every stage was her family, especially her sister Ethel, whose photographs from the mid-1930s reveal such happiness and purposefulness when they were in Rolvenden all too briefly together. Stoically, Dorothy had to cope with and get over a succession of setbacks, and her family's close support is an endearing aspect of this story.

Her pottery and all her achievements must have given her immense satisfaction, which was perhaps reflected in her charming expression when she was photographed by the *Kentish Express* just before she retired.

Reminiscing from the vantage point of time, forty five years after the pottery closed, Miss Pat Thoburn of Pympne Manor in Benenden, champion of local arts and crafts, who knew and supported Dorothy, wrote a fitting epitaph:

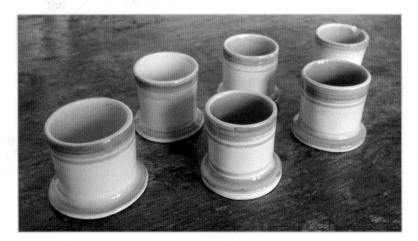

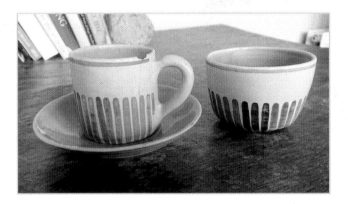

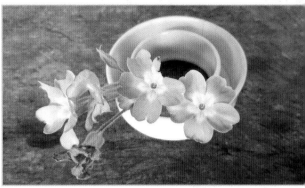

She always seemed a strong-minded person with well thought out and definitive views. She always wore the lovely blues and greens of her pottery!

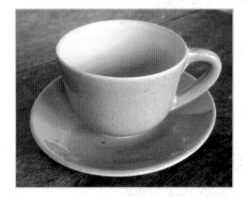

   I can now open the cupboards in the kitchen and there are still cups and saucers, the lovely striped cups and a saucer of the most beautiful blue glaze, and still in awe of green breakfast cups, egg cups and little dishes. They raise your spirits when you see them and use them, and it brings to mind a dedicated artist-potter. She most truly was a definitive figure in Rolvenden, and her artistic abilities entered many people's lives in bringing inspiration into all our ordinary days.

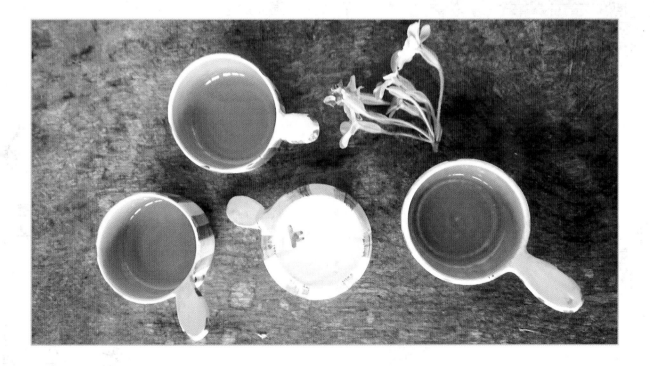

Picture Credits

Dorothy's sister, Ethel, was nicknamed 'Eb'.
Her photograph album is referred to as 'Eb's album'.
All photographs of Dorothy's pottery © Eula Mickelborg,
Purple Plum Photography, except where listed below.

Chapter 1
1 full page portrait of Dorothy © Paul Watson
2 *left top* Dorothy's mother © Paul Watson. *Left bottom* Dorothy's father courtesy of St Margaret's Church, Starston © William Barham. *Top right* 157 Chesterton Road, Cambridge © Paul Watson
3 *top* the Vicarage © unknown. *Bottom* St Mary's Church at Stow-cum-Quy © Landscape View Publishers, Market Harborough
4 family portraits, Eb's album © Paul Watson
5 *top left* St. Edward King and Martyr Church, Cambridge © unknown. *Top right* Reverend Canon Frederick Watson, and *bottom right* high altar at St. Edward King and Martyr © Paul Watson
6 6 Salisbury Villas, Cambridge, Eb's album © Paul Watson
7 family portraits, Eb's album © Paul Watson
8 family holiday in Hunstanton, Eb's album © Paul Watson
9 Dorothy after her father's death in 1906, Eb's album © Paul Watson
10 *top left* 12 Park Terrace in 1907, Eb's album © Paul Watson. *Top right* studio portrait of Dorothy © Paul Watson
11 *top* Dorothy in Canada in 1915, and *bottom* entrance to 'The Horseshoe Camp', Eb's album © Paul Watson
12 Basil Lockhart Watson and Dorothy J Chaffer © Paul Watson
13 Geoffrey and Ursula Watson, c. 1925 © Paul Watson

Chapter 2
15 Ravenscourt Pottery © Victoria and Albert Museum, London
16 Ravenscourt Pottery © Victoria and Albert Museum, London
17 Ravenscourt Pottery © Victoria and Albert Museum, London
18 Ravenscourt Pottery © Victoria and Albert Museum, London
19 Ravenscourt Pottery at a London fair © Victoria and Albert Museum, London
20 *top* Ravenscourt Pottery © Victoria and Albert Museum, London. *Bottom* Dorothy's Ravenscourt bowl © Arthur Watson's family

Chapter 3
23 C. H. Brannam and Sons Barnstaple Pottery wares © Richard Torrance
24 Sumner Place Mews © William Barham
28 Heal's catalogue © Victoria and Albert Museum, London
29 *top* horse-drawn delivery van © Historic England Archive. *Bottom* Sumner Place Mews © William Barham
30 Majel Davidson pictures courtesy of Heather Jack (2015) The Majel Davidson Archive and Object Collection, Scottish Pottery 26th Historical Review 2015 © Scottish Pottery Association
31 beaker in the possession of Majel Davidson. Picture credit © Heather Jack
32 Bridge Pottery mug, early 1920s © Richard Torrance
33 Careers for Women Pottery Making, *Morning Post*, October 13, 1926, Eb's scrapbook © Paul Watson

Chapter 4
36 Wentways Cottages, Eb's album © Paul Watson
37 family pictures, Eb's album © Paul Watson
38 family pictures, Eb's album © Paul Watson
40 *left* Heal's Presents catalogue © Victoria and Albert Museum, London
41 Bridge Pottery price lists, c. 1933 courtesy of Paul Watson
42 Sussex County Show promotional card courtesy of Paul Watson
46 *Hampshire Chronicle* Review, 8 August 1931, Eb's scrapbook © Paul Watson
47 *The Arts & Crafts Journal* article, Eb's scrapbook © Paul Watson
49 *Evening News and Southern Daily Mail* article, Eb's scrapbook © Paul Watson
52 extract from Jennifer's Notebook, *The Daily Mirror*, 1 December 1931, Eb's scrapbook © Paul Watson

Every effort has been made to identify and trace the
copyright owners of the images used in this publication.
YouByYou Books apologises for any inadvertent
infringement and invites copyright holders to make
contact if they believe their copyright has been infringed.

Acknowledgements

I am enormously grateful to Dorothy's great nephews, Paul and Stephen Watson and Richard Torrance, for all their material, help and encouragement with this work. Also, to Heather Jack, President of the Scottish Pottery Society whose interest in Dorothy comes through Majel Davison's Gushetneuk Pottery, for all her guidance. My thanks to Robert Corbett for sharing his knowledge about the Pottery in Beauworth, to Louise Chennell, Curator and Archivist of Ceramics at Aberystwyth, Jenna Rose and Sue Taylor of the Aberdeen Art Gallery, and the Allen Gallery of the Hampshire Cultural Trust in Alton.

I wish to thank Christopher Neve for his interest and support. Also, others around Rolvenden who knew Dorothy and have been able to contribute their recollections.

My appreciation to St John's College Cambridge, Cambridge County Archives, V&A Archive of Art & Design, Hole Park Estate, Michael Hook, Jackie King of Rolvenden History Society, Jo Carr of Wealden Pottery, Christopher Booth of Falstaff Motor Museum, and Tenterden Museum for their assistance. I am also most grateful to all who have allowed me to see and photograph their pottery collections and to the residents of Dorothy's former homes.

Finally, I wish to acknowledge the professional work by Anna Foster of YoubyYou Books, Alan Copps as editor, Eula Mickelborg of Purple Plum Photography, Alison Renno for the book design, and Ed Adams of Canterley Publishing towards the creation of this publication.

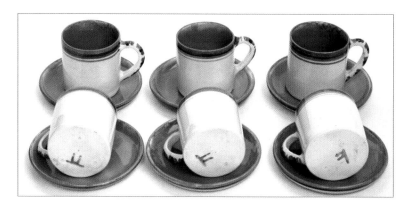

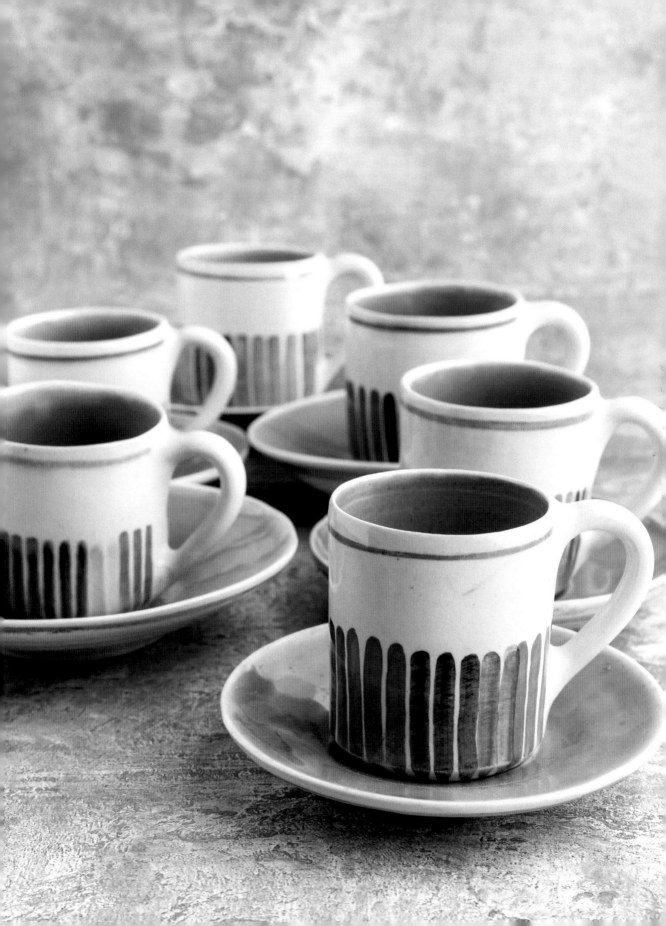